Hacking the IT Cube: The Information Technology Survival Guide.
By Douglas Chick

ISBN 0-9744630-2-7

Print 3

Publisher –TheNetworkAdministrator.com
201 W Cottesmore Cir
Longwood FL 32779

www.thenetworkadministrator.com

Janet Hays, Editor
Shelly Cox, Editor

Other books by Douglas Chick

 What All Network Administrators Know **ISBN:** 0974463000

 Steel Bolt Hacking **ISBN:** 0974463019

 Hacking the IT Cube: *The Information Technology Survival Guide* **ISBN:** 0974463027

 A Career in Computers...*without losing your MIND*
ISBN: 0974463035

Hacking the IT Cube:

The Information Technology Department Survival Guide

By Douglas Chick

Chapter 1: <u>Information Technologies 101</u>

Chapter 2:

<u>Positions in an IT Department</u>

Chapter 3:

When Looking for a Job

Chapter 4:
Hack / Anti Hacking Tools and Methods

Chapter 5:
Managing Your Network and Server Room

Chapter 6:
Managing an IT Department

Chapter 7:
Bitter Facts from Experiences

Appendix A

Appendix B

README.TXT

Hacking the Cube is a straightforward and sometimes comical look into the everyday world of information technology. It answers questions that many IT professionals and newcomers ask about the tools and skills needed to survive one of the most complex career fields in the world. Most computer books deal with configuring software and do little to help you learn what you need to know to work in a network office environment. Most people are unprepared for the social, political, or psychological aptitude needed to survive in the office workplace. The majority of computer books are software proprietary and they do not provide you with the necessary information on programs commonly found in the field of computers.

Many of the topics in this book are situations based on my experience and the experiences of other computer professionals that you would not typically have access to without actually having a job in an IT department. Other topics in this book are questions that have been e-mailed to my website, www.thenetworkadministrator.com, from people entering the information technology field for the first time. It also contains notes sent to me from well-established IT professionals about their experiences. This book is a mix of fact and story, humor and frustration. If you are new to the field of computers, Hacking the IT Cube is going to give you a unique insight that only experience can provide. On the other hand, if you are a seasoned veteran, you will laugh and cry at familiar situations that may have sent you to a place of liquid intoxication.

This book is written by a computer person for computer people and might not have some of the same nuances as a book written by a professional writer, such as proper structure, correct grammar, and a multi-million dollar support staff. I write from the experience of being on the job, and with a great deal of help from my friends, and spelling and grammar checker. I am an IT Director for a national company, and creator of a popular IT website. *Hacking the IT Cube* is an expanded edition of a much smaller issue titled, *What All Network Administrators Know*. With both books, I try to mix humor with textual fact to break up the monotonous boredom often associated with computer books.

For the newcomers, or those that are thinking about entering into a career with computers, do not allow any of the things I say to discourage you. I am merely trying to help you avoid some of the pitfalls and mistakes that I have seen, and some that I have made. Additionally, in terms of software knowledge, being a computer professional requires a great deal of acquired knowledge that you are not going to be able to learn overnight. <u>So remember,</u> nothing long lasting or worth having, such as a professional career, can happen overnight.

Chapter 1

Information Technologies 101

- ❏ A Word about Computer People
- ❏ Preparing for a Career in Computers
- ❏ Degree verses Computer Certifications
- ❏ Obtaining a Job without Experience
- ❏ Overlooking Inexperience
- ❏ Can I quit my job, go to a certification boot camp, and make 70K in 3 months
- ❏ Certification Resources
- ❏ Typing Skills
- ❏ How Much do Computer People Make
- ❏ Salaried Position

A Word about Computer People

The world of information technology is a strange and sometimes mysterious place to those that are on the outside. Computer people are smart, well trained, notoriously arrogant, and are responsible for the distribution of more gynecological imagery on the Internet than the mind can comfortably conceive.

In 2003, there were **25,007,505** reported businesses in the United States, with an estimated 98% using computers, which require a skilled computer person to repair, maintain, and manage their systems and operations. The U.S. Department of Labor, Bureau of Labor Statistics, reports that there are 2 million computer professionals in the U.S., with an estimated 200 million computers. This means that one computer person is responsible for 100 computers. However, the Department of Labor, Bureau of Labor Statistics, also reports that 5 % of the work force is home sick on a daily basis. This leaves 10,000,000 computers divided among the remaining workforces.

Two million hacking, cracking, Internet surfing, socially challenged techno-wizards are in charge of every database, e-mail server, web server, payroll system, bank, and airplane-controlling computer in the United States. There are computer people that use their powers for good, and those that use their powers for spam. We are a small group of professionals that are in charge of a large amount of important equipment. (In case, you forgot.) Another "interesting" statistic is that there are more people in North America with webbed toes than there are computer people and we are responsible for the data that drives the economy of the world. What do web-toed people contribute? It is not as if they are out there using their gifts winning gold medals in Olympic swim meets.

Preparing for a Career in Computers

There are certain requirements one must attend to before first applying for a job in a professional career. You must be educated, either through an institution (university, trade school, or junior college), self-educated, (books, Internet, home network) or from self-experience (talented liar). When there are not any jobs available after college, some people have no choice but to continue their education for another two years, and then two more. Some computer people spend up to 8-years in college before actually looking for a job. Many of those people simply become professors and teach the academics of what they learned in school. There are even others not comfortable with looking for a job unless they have every computer certification known to humankind behind their names.

> **John Doe,** *PhD, CCIE, CCNP, CCNA, CISSP, CCSP, MCSE, MCSA, MCSD, MCDBA, CAN, CDE, CIW, UNIX, Linux, Network+, A+...*

This is too many certifications just to tell people to reboot, check their printers for paper, and turn off their keyboard cap locks. Once you have the primary knowledge you need for a resume, the real job begins, looking for a job.

Certainly many books teach you about network protocols, configuring a database, writing and compiling the "Hello World" program in every programming language. Additionally, there are even more resources on how to write a great resume. After that, there seems to be a huge void of information that will tell you how to get a job, what to expect once you have a job, and how to keep it.

Nothing will impress a perspective employer more than experience. One year of experience is equal to 4 years of college. If you disagree with this, then you can argue the subject during your next job interview.

For those of you who want to enter into a career in computers, there is plenty of confusion about where to go and what to learn. This is especially true for those who want to become a Network Administrator. Colleges are not very specific when it comes to the computer sciences. They offer generalized degrees, not presenting an explicit career title. They may teach elements in basic networking, some programming, and quite a bit of desktop software instruction, however, none of which gives you enough insight into applying for a job for which you trained. The IT degree does not offer a career, just a field. Many graduates are on their own in finding a position within IT that they would like to pursue--even masters in computer logic and probabilities, or a PhD in probable fuzzy logic. What real career opportunities are there for people with nonsensical degrees? There are not any. This is why many people with higher degrees must teach. With respect to the many intelligent teachers and professors in the world, I have worked in a university's IT department and there is a huge disparity between teaching and doing. The difference with having experience is that it replaces what you have learned in the classroom and exercises your troubleshooting skills.

If universities really wanted to teach you a career in computers, there would be courses in printer repair and fax machines.
-- bitter network administrator

However, please understand me; you have a far better chance of getting a job with a degree than you would without one. I only mention this because, like computer certifications, many people believe because they have one; they expect to have immediate acceptance as an expert in the field. Do not allow that last statement to discourage you. Lack of experience does not mean that you will not get a job; it just means that you are not likely to get the top job, without first gaining a little experience. *Experience is the curse of the unemployed.* Every company has the position of Network Administrator; however, it is not a career position taught in school. There is no formal training to become a Network Administrator, because the job itself is a position of acquired skill and knowledge. *Simply put, it is a job of experience.* It is unlikely that a company will hire you as a Network Administrator right out of school. You do not have enough acquired knowledge to perform the job. You can, however, be hired on a helpdesk or as a network analyst or a systems analyst. These jobs are like an internship to becoming a Network Administrator or a Network Engineer. How long it takes you to become a Network Administrator or Network Engineer depends on how much time you are willing to invest in learning the key skills required to do the job. Database programmer is another example. Unless you are exceptionally talented, it is unlikely that a company will hire you out of school as a senior programmer to rewrite a mission critical database. To get the best job you can, you need to prepare yourself to the best of your ability.

Degree verses Computer Certifications

There are many computer people that have studied hard to collect the standard computer certifications, such as, an MCSE, CCNA or CCNP, Linux, Netware and a Unix certification. These are all good certifications to have, but remember, in today's job market, certifications are the basic minimum required by employers. Most positions require a degree as well as certifications. If you have the opportunity to go to a college or university then you need to do so. There are those that can just sneak by with a few certifications and land a high paying computer job, and many others that are extremely disappointed. If you are of the personality that is aggressive and smart, you will find a job in anything you seek, however, if you are the type of person that must rely on your credentials, you will need all the help you can get. Computer certifications without working experience are only a garnishment to a resume, therefore, you cannot rely on them to land you a job.

If you have just graduated high school and have the financial means to attend college but are undecided, you had better take my advice and get the degree. There are not many 17 to 21 year old computer professionals. Additionally, not having a degree hinders your ability to advance within a large corporate environment. You may very well sit on a help desk for four years and lose a promotion to Systems Engineer to a recent college graduate.

What happens if you do not have the resources to attend college? Will someone still want to hire you without a degree? Yes, and it happens every day. I taught myself, just as many of my friends have done. As I stated earlier, without a degree, our selections are limited. If one day you want to become a CIO (Chief Information Officer) or Vice President of Technology, you will be required to have a degree. As an IT Director, I might have to accept that, because I do not have a degree. Of course, if this sounds like a path you will take, you will discover other options in the course of your career and being a CIO will not really matter.

However, I know plenty of people that are self-taught, self-studied for their certifications, and they are working in the industry today. You just have to be dedicated and self-disciplined. If you do not have these two traits, you are going to have to learn them or lessons will be long and slow for you. When people ask me how I learned computers or networking, I like to tell them, "I taught myself. Because I didn't know much to begin with, lessons were long and slow and the instructor wouldn't stop talking about himself."

Many employers place a great deal of value in someone that is self-taught. I know a woman named Ellen that is a good example of this. She quit her job, dedicated herself to doing nothing but learning networking, self-studied, and in two months, she got an MCSE. In her first week, she had five interviews; four with Microsoft and received four offers. She chose the job with Cisco Routers on the Microsoft backbone in Redmond, Washington. Dave, her boss, picked her because of her drive and determination and her ability to learn. It took her another five years before she ever looked at a local area network. I always choose someone with a positive attitude and the aggressiveness to learn above anyone else. I will always hire someone eager without experience over someone lackluster with experience.

When I review a resume, the first thing that I look at is what software knowledge is listed. There are many instances when a network manager or an IT Director needs someone with knowledge that falls just below a certain salary level. The problem with hiring someone with too much experience is he or she often comes with higher salary requirements and bad work habits. Sometimes it is better to hire someone smart and eager who just needs a break. You will find that most employers think in these same terms. Managers who do not agree with this philosophy will never call you based on your resume in the first place, so you will never have to address their issues with inexperienced workers. If you only have self-experience to offer a potential employer, be confident enough in what you have listed on your resume to do the job. When you submit a resume, you are telling a potential employer that *you have done the best you can on your own, to make yourself ready for this position.*

Obtaining a Job <u>Without</u> Experience?

One of the greatest things about having a computer job is; someone pays you to obtain enough experience to find a better one.
-- I said that.

No one is born with experience, except for maybe the French...and civil servants. Besides these two groups, no one else is born with working job experience. Everyone has had a job without prior experience at least once; and you will too. Worrying whether or not you can get a job without experience is foolish; worrying about getting a 200K per year job without experience is also foolish, because it will not happen. (At least there is a high enough probability that it is unlikely.)

--Anyone that has ever had a job was hired at least one time in his or her life without some form of job experience.

Starting at the Top

Many people have been convinced that if they get a degree or certain certifications they will obtain a top-paying job in a company of their choosing. *God bless your naive little hearts.* I am not saying that it is not possible. With the "right" last name and from the "right" school, you could be president of the United States, but you had better have great connections, because a corporation is not as likely to start you at the top, as an elected office will. Even Bill Gates and Paul Allen started at the bottom. I mean, granted they started from a higher altitude, but it was still a bottom position.

Because I hear so many IT managers complain about a young, just out of school candidate, or someone with a boot camp certification, enter an interview with a list of demands, I feel it is an important issue to address. I even interviewed a young man one time, with no experience, first time job. When I asked if he had any questions, he replied that he wanted a new laptop, a credit card, and asked about a company car. I saved him the embarrassment of failing the company drug test.

Overlooking Inexperience

Product knowledge is the key to overcoming lack of experience. Computer programs create computer careers. Software companies create programmers, network administrators, SQL programmers, and router administrators. Inexperience is secondary if you know the product. In other words, product knowledge is an acceptable replacement for experience. Product knowledge can be described as knowing an operating system, a programming language, a router OS, or an SQL language inside and out. While studying C++, I was talking to a Vice President at Microsoft, and he asked me how well I knew C++? He needed C++ programmer's right then. He knew I had no programming experience but he was willing to overlook it, if I was eager and knowledgeable enough to use the product. I was not, and subsequently he did not pursue it any further.

You can also gain knowledge from self-experience. Self-experience sounds a lot like what lonely people do, but in this context, self-experience can be setting up networks and servers from your home or a lab. Self-experience can be labeled as writing computer programs on your own. Simply put, self-experience is when you teach yourself, either from a school or from home product knowledge. When real experience is not available, you just have to do the next best thing.

Product knowledge is the most important tool you can have when looking for a job, whether you are a seasoned professional or just starting out. A degree in computer science is a nice adornment on a resume, but it does little to help you get a job without some type of software knowledge.

Every time that you install a network operating system, create a user account, or set up a DNS, DHCP, WINS, or Print Server, you have that knowledge to use at a later time. Many people tell me that they cannot learn out of a book, they can only learn from hands-on work. It is true that it is difficult to retain computer knowledge when you read it from a book. I have difficulty learning from a book unless I can apply the knowledge to a specific task. Sometimes what does not seem to make much sense in a book, will one day suddenly make a lot of sense the first time you have to apply it.

Reading a book about computers or computer programs is an acquired skill. Readers have compared the experience to watching senior citizens play golf. Computer books are dry, uninteresting, and often require the reader to keep a festering open wound so that he or she may continually jab at it to stay awake. Many new people never make it past the first 50 pages of a computer book, (also known as the wall). Because of this, they never pursue a career in computers. It is my theory that these first 50 pages are specifically designed to prevent an over population in the field of computers. These pages include a review of the history and creation of the subject matter and gives credit to all of the principle parties that have in some way contributed to the program or protocol in question. Also included is the description of how to use the book, who should read it, the type of paper used to create the book, and how many stitches are in the binding. Last, but not least, on the fiftieth page is a section dedicated to conventions that are used in understanding the book that are almost immediately forgotten the moment they are read. Those that are computer professionals today, had the instinct to flip past the first 50 pages, and therefore not subjected to the mind numbing characterless beginnings that plague every computer book. In case you were wondering, I eliminated these first 50 pages.

I know that I wandered away a bit from the subject, but I am trying to sneak in the answers to other questions that are typically associated to this one. So yes, you can get a job without experience, but it does not mean you can get away without learning how to do the job.

While we are here, I will quickly address another question that I am always asked:

Can I quit my job, go to a certification boot camp and make 70K in 3 months?

No.

This is a troubling question, and I get it quite a bit. Junior colleges and certification boot camps advertise that you can change your career within 6 to 8 weeks, receive a certification and make over 50K a year right out of the blocks. I was in a bookstore, when a man standing in front of the MCSE certification section, explained to me that he qualified for a government grant to get an MCSE. He said he was going to quit his job in advertising and make more money in the computer field. I tried to explain to him that it might not be that easy, because the tech sector is suffering from the economy, and if he already has a job, he might want to think about keeping it. He gave me a dirty look and wandered away with a $200.00 set of certification books. I should have never broached my opinion on the subject. People never listen anyway. **But**, the chances of a 50-year old man or woman, starting without any computer knowledge, and then getting a quick certification to a high paying career in computers, is not very likely.

If a certification boot camp or learning institution tells you that after taking their course, you can get an instant, high paying career in anything, you should at least be a little suspicious. If they had any credibility at all, they could furnish you with a list of successful candidates. In fact, should not most or all of their graduating classes already be making big money in computers?

Ask yourself how many jobs there are in the world that starts out with an inexperienced worker at the top, not very many.

Look at the employment section of your local paper and tell me how many legitimate jobs are listed that state:

Wanted: no experience necessary. With only 6 weeks of education to pass a test, we will hire you to manage all the servers, workstations, and network in our company. You only need to apply with a certification and a note from your instructor that states you were a good test taker.

Just be careful when people tell you what certifications can do. The certification freight train has already left the station. A great deal of money has been made by companies that promised a computer certification would get you a great job, and because of this, they saturated the market with unskilled, highly certified workers that cannot find work.

Without work experience, certifications only compliment your actual product knowledge. Most IT job interviews include a technical interview that includes very specific questions about your product knowledge. If you cannot answer basic questions or perform specific tasks, you will not pass the interview. I know network managers who will end the interview immediately if someone answers technical questions with, "I'm certified in it, aren't I?" Very few people are capable of faking a technical interview. If you are someone that can, you may skip this section and go straight to, "How long should I hold out before accepting the job?" (Note: there is not really a section titled, "How long should I hold out before accepting the job?")

During an interview, you should tell the interviewer just what you know, how you earned it, *that you have done all you can to teach yourself, and now you are looking for an opportunity to learn first hand.* Network Managers and IT Directors are so gun shy, that if you cannot answer their questions, then this is the only answer they want to hear. A certification will not hold up in a job interview, if you did not retain the data necessary to pass the course. If reading this makes you nervous, you need to go back to the books and set up as many different networks as you can. At the bare minimum, you must at least be able to do what you have listed on your resume. If self-experience is the only thing you can offer, you had better be good at it. Network Analyst, System Analyst, and Helpdesk Technicians are all positions that are available without prior experience. These positions give you an opportunity to gain first hand experience on a network server, workstations, and even in the server room.

Certification Resources

The following resources have helpful information regarding certifications and training.

http://www.Brainbench.com/
http://www.Mcpmag.com/
http://www.Certmag.com/
http://www.CramSession.com/

Beware of brain dumps. Certification brain dumps are websites where test takers share their test results, questions, and answers. Brain dumps are not a reliable source of information and if caught using one, you can lose your certifications.

IT Tip

Typing Skills

It is an odd thing, but your typing skills may determine your abilities and experience level as seen by others. Immediately upon entering the computer field, I noticed that I was looked down upon because I used the hunt and peck method of typing. Someone who makes a career on instruments that use a keyboard as its primary input device should master such a device. It is like turning your car over to a mechanic who does not know how to use a wrench properly. To overcome this, I practiced using a typing program for 30 minutes a night for one month, and at the end of the month, I could type 60 words a minute. Computer professionals type, not hunt and peck. Poor keyboard skills stand out.

How Much Do Computer People Make?

The number one question I receive on my website is; *how much do computer people make*? The very first thing you should know, never trust those lying "Salary Surveys" posted on the Internet. I have been in salary negotiations where the person brought one of those salary surveys, and declared that they should be making the industry standard. They stated that if their salary did not meet industry standards, they were going to quit. That survey cost *Poindexter* his job that day, as my boss told him that we did not want to hold anyone back from fulfilling his or her potential. Pride forced *Poindexter* to walk out and stupidity caused him to trust a salary survey. I later convinced my boss, who was the CEO of the company, to take *Poindexter* back, but it cost him a week's worth of wages and another year to get a reasonable raise.

I determined one time that for a salary survey to be accurate in my area, at least one computer person had to make 8 million dollars a year to average out the survey's numbers.

Another mistake made by job applicants in today's job market is that they are demanding too much money when he or she has no experience. There was a time that you could graduate from college or acquire several certifications, with no experience, and demand big wages. That ship sailed to India. Unless you can offer a company something that no one else can, you better be humble, appreciative, and look for an opportunity to test what you have learned, so you can gain experience. Why is that? Because you are in competition with a multitude of others willing to work cheaper just to get a shot at earning experience, and attitude means everything. I know five IT Directors right now that would disqualify you in an instant just for being too cocky or that you overstate your knowledge because you have a few certifications.

A Network Administrator makes on the average anywhere between $40,000 and $75,000 a year. Helpdesk technicians and programmers rate a different range. Because every area of the world has a different local economy, it is impossible for me to tell you how much you can make. The best source of how much money you can make in your area is to search the job market online, either at **www.monster.com, www.dice.com, www.hotjobs.com** or through your local newspaper's employment ads. This is also a good reference to find out what software you should know as well.

Spoiled in the past with high wages, so many computer people allow their pride to get in the way and not accept anything less than what they were making before. If you can get a job—take it! Remember, it is easier to get a job when you already have one, then to find one when you are desperate and behind on paying your bills.

Salaried Position

Generally, IT positions are salaried. Why is that? Because IT people often have to work many nights, weekends, and employers do not want to pay for it, so you must manage your time wisely. Sometimes, no matter how well you manage your time, you are just going to have work late. Viruses are probably the number one cause for your unpaid overtime hours. This is why so many Network Administrators want to form a vigilante militia to hunt virus makers and hackers and dole out our own brand of justice. I am not sure what that is exactly, but it will be severe. Viruses are not the only reason for unpaid overtime hours; upgrades, updates, new install, server crashes, and service packs. There are critical security patches, more security patches, and even more security patches and do not forget about those critical security patches, because if you are not up on those babies, it is back to viruses and hackers.

Years ago, when I had to have stitches in my hand, the doctor turned towards me with a needle and said, "It is going to hurt and that's just the way it is." I smiled because I thought he was kidding...filthy animal.

It is the same with being a salaried IT worker; sometimes it is just going to hurt, but there are so many other benefits in the computer department that the occasional late night install does not matter.

Chapter 2

Positions in an IT Department

- ❏ Helpdesk Phone Support
- ❏ Helpdesk Technician
- ❏ Network Analyst
- ❏ Network Administrator
- ❏ Network Engineer
- ❏ Network Security Administrator
- ❏ Database Administrators
- ❏ Webmaster
- ❏ Programmers
- ❏ IT Consultants
- ❏ Director of Information Technology
- ❏ Chief Information Officer

IT Positions

IT departments will vary on how they determine the title of a position, which can cause confusion. Examples of this are the titles, Helpdesk Technician and Support Technician. Both jobs perform the same task but have different names. In this section, I have compiled a list of typically used job titles, needed education, associated skills, and duties.

- Helpdesk Phone Support
- Helpdesk Technician
- Network Analyst
- Network Administrator
- Network Engineer
- Network Security Specialist
- E-mail Administrator
- Database Administrator
- Web Designer
- Web Developer
- Programmer
- IT Consultant
- Director of Information Systems (IT Manager)
- Chief Information Officer

Helpdesk Phone Support (Phone Support Analyst, Support Services, Phone Support Engineer)

When the statement "**Click Here**" is difficult to understand, when "**Press Any Key**" does not provide enough options, and when you are not quite sure if you should say yes to "**Format Hard Drive Now,**" the helpdesk support hotline is there for you.

To be a Phone Support Engineer, you must be a kind and understanding person, enjoy people, and have the psychic ability to read minds. You must also have strong translation skills. You have to be able to translate the word 'thingy," into its hardware or software equivalent, that can change between computer terms within seconds. Patience is the key to computer phone support. If you are not a patient person, you should not consider this as a long-time career goal.

Helping people with their computer problems by phone is far more difficult than in person. Talking someone through something as simple as a *right click* of the mouse can be misinterpreted as *writing* the word *click*. *Right Click* can equal *Write Click*, C: prompt can be *Sea-prompt*, and *Reboot* can be turn off your monitor. Proper communication is the key to working a helpdesk support line; this also means that you must translate your language into what stupid people can understand.

Education

A college degree is not typically required for this type of computer position, although certifications can be a plus. A helpdesk support person may even have an A+ or Microsoft Office certification. A helpdesk tech usually learns his or her technical skills on the job. Their support ranges from e-mail, MS Office, to connectivity issues. Most companies also have their own priority software, which the helpdesk also supports.

The helpdesk is generally an entry-level position and in many cases, a base launching point into other IT career levels. It is common to see newly graduated IT majors beginning their careers at the helpdesk. It is my opinion that every computer person should spend time on the helpdesk.

Associated Skills

Service packs and security updates: Systems that are not up-to-date on service packs and security updates are not only a threat to their own normal operations, but to everyone in the company. Even though updates do not keep out all pests, they do keep out all known pests. After all, no one wants to fight yesterday's fires.

Printer error troubleshooting: With this type of computer position, be aware that you will receive many calls concerning printer problems. Jammed paper, (feeder roller or tray problem) out of ink, cannot connect to printer (check cable or network connections); these are all typical user problems which you will be required to resolve.

Monitor problems: Intermittent flickering of monitor, missing colors, black screen; these are also common problems associated with monitor errors.

Hard drive problems: Hard drive making a clicking sound, (step up barring or motor failure) missing folders, foreign and ineligible characters replace file or folder names. Not all hard drives suddenly crash and stop working. In many cases, a hard drive will show signs that it is having trouble.

RAM (memory) problems: Low ram can cause a multitude of problems if too many programs are running at once. Ad ware and viruses will also cause memory shortages.

Internet connections: Loss of Internet connection is always a favorite on the helpdesk. You must look at cable connections, IP address status, or wrong user names.

Operating systems: Desktop operating systems are company specific. Some companies may still employ Windows NT workstations, while others may be up-to-date with the current OS. I have seen OS2, Mac, Linux, Unix, Windows NT 4, Windows 95, 98, Millennium, 2000, and XP. Only experience can give you knowledge of the many operating systems available.

From TheNetworkAdministrator.com...

Terms and Comprehension

The most difficult part of any computer support is the misuse of the terms that computer people use, and their meanings according to the computer user. Here are several misunderstood computer terms by the computer end-user.

Your Understanding	Their Understanding
Backup: data being backed up to storage device.	**Backup**: The opposite of go forward.
Cursor: Flashing pointer positioning.	**Cursor**: A rap artist
Dump: Server Blue Screen	**Dump:** A Network Administrator's work area
Defrag: Defragmentation collects streams of data and stores it together on the hard disk.	**Defrag:** What some religious groups claim they can accomplish with counseling.
Dongle: A device that prevents the unauthorized use of hardware or software.	**Dongle**: Something that if touched in front of an end-user, may cause a sexual harassment lawsuit.
DSL: Digital subscriber lines up to 1.5 mbps	**DSL**: Cable Modem
Modem: A modem is device that converts computer data into sound that can be transmitted over phone lines.	**Modem**: Computer case, hard drive, monitor, motherboard, mouse, keyboard, a sound that cats make while in heat.

E-mail: Electronic mail	**E-mail**: A medium used to send cat pictures to friends that cannot have children
Emoticon: :-)	**Emoticon:** Geeks that cannot express feelings
Encryption: Encryption is the process of changing data into a form that can be read only by the intended receiver.	**Encryption:** A language used to explain computer problems to end-users.
FAT: file allocation table	**FAT:** The AP department of every company in the world and many programmers as well.
Fat binary: Large files that Macintosh and Power Mac can send.	**Fat binary:** A very large single digit that is typically used while driving behind the elderly.
Flash ROM: Reprogramming a new BIOS	**Flash ROM:** What I am going to do if I get fired.
Ghosting: Copying a hard drive sector by sector	**Ghosting:** What I am going to do if I am fired.
Gigabyte: 1,073,741,824 bytes	**Gigabyte:** Why Herb Albert went to court.
Gopher: Helpdesk Engineer.	**Gopher:** An accounting clerk.
Phong shading: In 3D graphics, the polygons that make up the graphics need to be shaded.	**Phong shading:** When you want to wear a thong, but only have a black magic marker.
Ping: Packet Internet Groper	**Ping:** The sound that the monitor makes when users bump their head against the glass.

POP: Post Office Protocol	**POP:** The sound that is made the second time their head hits the monitor.
PPP: point-to-point protocol	**PPP:** What happens if they drink too much coffee
Public domain: Food in the lunch room refrigerator after 12:30 PM	**Public domain:** Food in the lunch room refrigerator after 12:30 PM
RAID: redundant array of independent (or inexpensive) disks	**RAID**: Going through your desk after we fix your computer.
RAM: random access memory	**RAM**: Male sheep
Resolution: *Resolution* is a measure of graphics that is used to describe what a printer can print.	**Resolution**: To quit smoking and lose weight after the holidays.
Twisted pair: Telephone companies commonly run twisted pairs of copper wires to each customer household	**Twisted pair:** When a computer geek marries the graphic artist in marketing.
TWAIN: Scanner driver	**TWAIN:** Another word for locomotive.

Helpdesk Technician (Helpdesk Engineer, Customer Support, Helpdesk Analyst)

Those who have worked in a helpdesk position and survived, compare the experience to working in a mental asylum for the criminally insane, but much, much, worse. It is worse because in a mental asylum, you can sometimes get the occasional hug shortly after morning meds. Not to say that you will not get the occasional hug in the office workplace—you will—but it is a brief encounter that only occurs after removing a jammed piece of paper from the printer.

Seriously, a well-trained helpdesk, that is to say, a helpdesk that has trained their computer users well, will not have near the problems as a department that has not. By trained, I mean that you must create procedures and strictly maintain them. If you allow people to call or come to your office with every problem, the job can quickly become chaotic and too overwhelming to handle.

Helpdesk Queue

Many helpdesks deploy some type of helpdesk form that allows their users to file requests that go into a queue. In my opinion, this is the best method to use. Using a database (MySQL, Access), a scripting language (PHP, ASP, Perl), and a Web program, (Apache, IIS...etc) you can develop your own.

Any program that allows users to enter their problem into a database and return a report number to them through e-mail, or the web page itself, is a good program. (You might even want the e-mail or web page to have a few helpful suggestions while waiting, such as; reboot, cap locks, add paper.)

I visited one large company and was surprised to find a clipboard on a hook. If a computer user had a problem, they would walk up and write in their name, station number, problem, and time. I find this method to be extremely disorganized and difficult to track.

Organization is the key to keeping you and your company's computer users from becoming frustrated. I have seen an entire billing department go home because someone said that their billing program would be down for the entire day, when in fact it was only down for 20 minutes. Once the database was up again, they did not want to be the only department working, and forfeited 7 hours worth of pay.

If they have to follow a queue system, and they receive confirmation that their complaints were processed, then they are happy to wait for a resolution to their problem. However, if they just send an e-mail or put their name on the list without some form of reciprocation, within minutes, they will become stressed, and in many cases, angry. **An angry computer user is a crazed one.**

Helpdesk Software

- QuickLogs: http://www.quicklogs.com/
- Helpdesk Reporter: http://www.helpdeskreporter.com/
- Trouble Ticket Management: http://e11online.com/
- Helpdesk Pro: http://www.helpdeskpro.net/
- MagicIT: http://www.remedy.com/solutions/magic/
- BridgeTrak: http://www.kemma.com/

Education

A college degree is helpful in any career field; however, it is not necessary to gain employment as a helpdesk technician. Experience and certifications are useful in this position. A+,

MCP, Network+, and a Novell's CNA would be particularly helpful as a Helpdesk Technician.

Associated Skills

Hardware trouble-shooting basics: In any computer-related field, it is always a good idea to learn the hardware basics. Because hardware drives the software of a computer, it is difficult to trouble-shoot a computer problem without proper hardware knowledge.

Network configuration: Because most office software connects to a network database, you must at least learn how to configure a desktop's network options, more specifically, TCP/IP setting. Learn the uses for DHCP, DNS, ODBC, and default gateway settings. Learn how to trouble-shoot network connectivity. In addition, you should learn logon profiles and their application in a corporate environment. Mapping network drives is a common practice as a Helpdesk Tech, as well.

Network hardware basics: Learn basic network equipment uses and configurations, such as network cards, hubs, switches, bridges, and routers.

Printer installation: Printer "problems" are a major issue in any office environment. The person in this computer position should already have a good understanding of configuration and installations.

Viruses: Helpdesk Technicians are on the front line with computer viruses. Depending upon the anti-virus system, the Helpdesk Tech removes viruses, adware, and general malware.

Service packs and security updates: Systems that are not up-to-date on service packs and security updates are not only a threat to their own normal operations, but to everyone in the company. Even though updates do not keep out all pests, they do keep out all known pests. After all, no one wants to fight yesterday's fires.

Repairing PCs and building Clones: Helpdesk Techs are often required to handle hardware repairs and build clone PCs from the ground up. This is where an A+ certification can come in handy.

Desktop applications: Trouble-shooting e-mail, word processing, spreadsheet programs, databases connections, and Internet browser's applications are everyday occurrences.

The Blame Game

Creditability, integrity, and accountability are three important human traits that you will not find in politics, or the office workplace. From the CEO down to the ranks of the lowly office clerk, no one is willing to be accountable for anything. No other department is as sensitive to this problem as the computer department. If an accountant deletes a spreadsheet and you have a nightly backup, then there should have been an hourly backup. Another action that you will see working in an IT department, is the fear associated with a computer problem. In almost every case, even at the executive level, even from your boss, even from the CEO of the company, when you show up to fix a computer problem, the user first apologizes and then begins telling you that it was not their fault. A helpdesk position can be a first stage building block in helping enhance the self-esteem of a computer geek.

Although I should add that from time to time, some people will actually admit they must have done something wrong. This type of response is extremely rare and often causes a tear to well up in your eye.

Most company computer users, no matter how miniscule the problem, are afraid they will be blamed for breaking the computer. They are quick to tell you that they did not cause the problem. Then they will spend the next 30 minutes (if you let them), explaining what they think the problem is, and finally closing with how they hate computers *and it is your fault*. Like the person in a complaints department, a computer person must be thick-skinned. Blaming the IT department for every computer problem is just part of the problem and those that cannot adjust usually find another career quickly.

The Magic of Reboot

Computer programmers and computer users alike both believe that "reboot" is the lazy IT department's way of fixing every computer problem, and in many respects, this is true. The view from a Helpdesk Tech is this: most helpdesks are under-manned, and there is just not enough time to sit at a computer and try to figure out what the user or user's programs are doing wrong to cause the computer to freeze. In most causes, it is a simple matter of too many programs jockeying for position on the computers RAM. Most companies purchase their computers in bulk, or from the lowest bid, which usually results in sacrificing performance. (RAM, CPU speed, video card, network card...you get it). In many large companies, the act of adding more memory or upgrades to a computer almost requires an Act of Congress (without the pork projects).

Step 1.→ The Helpdesk Tech makes a request through the *Network Administrator*, for additional RAM for Alice in the *Billing Department*. The Network Administrator looks it over, fills out a purchase order, signs it, and then passes it up to his or her boss; the *Director of Information Technology*.

Step 2.→ The purchase order goes to the *Director of Information Technology* for his or her approval. The director looks it over, agrees or disagrees, and the purchase order is then sent to someone in *budget*.

Step 3. → A clerk in "budget" looks over the purchase order, associates it to the department that will receive the RAM, sends a copy of the purchase order to the head of that department, and waits for an approval.

Step 4. → The department head looks over the request, glances at the price, gets up and walks over to the person whose computer is freezing up, and asks Alice if they really need to spend $50 of their budget on RAM. Alice gets nervous, says that she is not really having a problem, and the P.O. is rejected.

Alice continues to have a problem and complains bitterly that the IT department is incompetent.

Scenario 1.2:

Alice: "The thing that you added to my computer didn't work. My computer is frozen again. I'm getting very aggravated with this, Gerald!" (Gerald is the name of our example helpdesk person.)

Helpdesk: "What were you doing when your computer froze?"

Alice: "What was I doing? Why, I wasn't doing anything—it just froze!"

(At this point, Alice has fallen into a defensive position.)

Helpdesk: "I wasn't suggesting that you did anything wrong, I'm just trying to troubleshoot the problem."

Alice: "The problem is you put more RAM in my modem, instead of fixing the real problem!"

(Alice has quickly turned her frustration into anger and directed it towards Gerald. Additionally, company computer users always call their computer case a modem, or CPU. I do not know why; they are just stupid.)

Helpdesk: "…"

(Immediately Gerald has felt Alice's anger and he becomes angry. Instead of lashing back at her, he calms the situation by saying…"

Helpdesk: "I think there is cake in the lunch room."

Alice: "Cake?"

Helpdesk: "I think it's your boss' birthday—her 50th?"

Alice: "Oh no…umm, I'll just reboot and get back to you later."

Alice runs off in a frantic tizzy, thinking she has forgotten her boss' birthday and is now rushing into her office to wish her a happy 50th birthday. Gerald, a seasoned helpdesk tech, avoided a hostile confrontation that could have potentially gotten him written up, and instead sent Alice to her boss' office where she made a complete and utter fool of herself by wishing her 40-year- old boss a happy birthday.

It is difficult to diagnose *"Frozen Users Computer Kiosk Syndrome"* because any combination of events could cause a computer to freeze. *Frozen Users Computer Kiosk Syndrome* can be caused by two programs trying to use the same register in the CPU or Memory space, program error, or even little kitty dancing across the computer monitor at the exact instant a mission critical process was trying to update the user's database.

Like in a hospital emergency room, the computer helpdesk is a difficult environment to work because you only work with people that are in pain. By the time they contact you, they are aggravated, irritable, and difficult to handle. Frequently, I have a pep talk with my helpdesk staff, reassuring them that humanity is worth saving…but not all of it.

Network Analyst (Network Specialist, Support Technician, LAN Support)

A Network Analyst is somewhere between the helpdesk and the Network Administrator. This position supports computer users, helpdesk staff, and the Network Administrator. Network Analysts work on special projects. The projects assigned to Network Analysts can be computer rollouts, the deployment of a videoconference system, or the current project at hand. A Network Analyst usually has a specific network segment to manage as well as a territory. In this position, you can build stronger server and networking skills that will help you advance to a Network Administrator.

Duties assigned to a Network Analyst:

- Backups
- Server service packs and security updates
- Network equipment support
- Network monitoring
- Systems utilization reporting
- Traffic shaping
- Systems and license auditing
- Desktop and network equipment maintenance
- Inventory

Education

A college degree is helpful in any career field. The more education and certifications you have, the more likely you will be able to obtain a job as a Network Analyst. Many IT graduates begin as a Network Analyst and obtain their experience to move on to higher-level computer jobs.

An IT, MIS, or Computer Science degree is the preferred college degree, however many computer people may have other types of degrees that are completely unrelated to computers. I know of many IT people with engineering degrees, degrees in physics, and even graphic design. It is common to get to the last year of college and realize that you would rather work with computers. My department once hired a recent graduate as a Webmaster, with a degree in fisheries. He later moved on to become an SQL admin for Microsoft.

Some of the certifications helpful to this position; A+, Network+, Server +, Microsoft's MCP, MCSE, Novell's CNA, Cisco's CCNA, or CCNP.

Associated Skills

Hardware trouble-shooting basics: In any computer related field, it is always a good idea to learn the hardware basics. Because hardware drives the software of a computer, it is difficult to trouble-shoot a computer problem without proper hardware knowledge.

Network configuration: Because most office software connects to a network database, you must already know how to configure a desktop's network options. You should know how to configure the client side of ODBC connections, DHCP, DNS, and know the uses for a default gateway. Additionally, as a Network Analyst, you may need to configure a DHCP, DNS server. You should also know by now how to map network drives at the GUI and command line level.

User Management: How to manage user profiles, logons, and home directories.

Network hardware: It is common for a Network Analyst to work beside a network administrator or network engineer, along with the installation and configuration of a variety of network appliances, such as network cards, hubs, switches, bridges and routers.

Printer installation: Printer "problems" are a major issue in any office environment. Drives become corrupt, rollers always need replaced, and of course—paper jams. As a Helpdesk Tech, you are already familiar with how to install printers to a desktop and how to map to network shared printers. In the position of Network Analyst, you may need to install network printers using TCP/IP, DLC, and other network protocols.

Viruses: A Network Analyst often moves from fighting viruses from the desktop to the server enterprise level. Many IT departments employ the use of an anti-virus program that scans and manages anti-virus software from a centralized location, such as a server. This eliminates the need to install anti-virus software on each desktop personally. Enterprise software will push the software onto the computers that you direct to receive it.

Service packs and security updates: Systems that are not up-to-date on service packs and security updates are not only a threat to their own normal operations, but to everyone in the company. Even though updates do not keep out all pests, they do keep out all known pests. After all, no one wants to fight yesterday's fires. Because of this, it is important to make sure your servers and workstations are up-to-date on their patches. Most computer systems can be configured to update patches at a predetermined time without the aid of the IT department having to update manually every system, everyday. However, it is often necessary to check to see if your machines are doing what they were configured to do.

Repairing PCs and building Clones: Helpdesk techs, Network Analysts, and Network Administrators are often required to provide hardware repairs and build clone PCs from the ground up.

Network Administrator (Systems Administrator, LAN Admin, Server Admin)

Being a Network Administrator is a lot like being an African Rhinoceros; you have to be thick skinned, have keen listening skills, and have the ability to rush in and put out fires. (Rhinoceros are sometimes known to charge into campsites and stomp out campfires.) Another similarity between Network Administrators and the Rhinoceros is the fact they are tracked in the wild, but instead of being ear tagged or radio collared; computer people are impaled with cell phones and pagers. The difference between the two species is that if you wake a Rhinoceros at 6 a.m. asking if the e-mail server is down, the Rhino will most probably kill you, whereas a Network Administrator will only wish death upon you.

A Network Administrator is typically in charge of a company's local area network, but in mid to small sized companies, a Network Administrator is the local and wide area network admin, e-mail admin, Webmaster, database admin, SQL admin, security admin, helpdesk support, and company trainer. The Network Administrator is responsible for every computer, workstation, server, network node and protocol that connects to his or her network. Additionally, a Network Administrator is responsible for printer services, documentation, network performance, and disaster plan and recovery on a host of multi-platform operating systems from software manufacturers that hate each other. The Network Administrator is often in charge of the company's phone system as well.

A Network Administrator is a title of acquired experience. In other words, a Network Administrator receives his or her training from hands-on experience. A Network Administrator is often referred to as a generalist, because the job requires general knowledge in almost every function within the IT department. Every other IT position depends, in some way or another, on the Network Administrator for permissions, configurations, and connectivity.

Education and Certifications

A college degree is usually required but not necessarily mandatory, depending upon the right candidate. The position of Network Administrator is a position of acquired experience, however, the more education and certifications you have; the easier it is for you to obtain a job. An ideal candidate would be one that has worked their way up from other IT positions until they acquired enough on-the-job training to manage their own network and server room.

In this career position, a Network Administrator would have obtained as many network certifications as he could. Some of the main certifications obtained by a Network Administrator are Microsoft's MCP, MCSE, Linux Administrator, Novell's CNA, Cisco's CCNA, or CCNP. Most Network Administrators are well rounded and have Microsoft SQL or Oracle cert, an E-mail server certification such as Microsoft Exchange, and even a programming language.

Associated Skills

Server and network appliance hardware: Network administrators work with server hardware more than desktop IDE components. SCSI hard drives, controllers, RAID controllers, backup drives, storage devices, firewalls, routers, and dual CPU sets.

Network configuration: E-mail servers, SQL servers, Print and file servers, DHCP, DNS, Active directory, Virtual Private Networks, TCP/IP suite of tools, Wireless networks, Hubs, Switches, firewalls, routers, NFS, SNMP, AppleTalk.

User Management: The Network Administrator is responsible for creating user names and passwords, user profiles, logons, and home directories. Additionally, the Network Administrator is responsible for the computer naming convention. That is the style of names used to name a company's servers and workstations.

Printer installation: Printer "problems" are a major issue in any office environment. Drives become corrupt, rollers always need replaced, and of course—paper jams. As a Network Administrator, you are already familiar with how to install printers to a desktop, and how to map to network shared printers. In the position of Network Analyst, you may need to install network printers using TCP/IP, DLC, and other network protocols.

Viruses: A Network Administrator fights viruses from the server enterprise level. Many IT departments employ the use of an anti-virus program that scans and manages anti-virus software from a centralized location, such as a server. This eliminates the need to install anti-virus software on each desktop personally. Enterprise software will push the application onto the computers from one central location without visiting each computer.

Service packs and security updates: Systems that are not up-to-date on service packs and security updates are not only a threat to their own normal operations, but to everyone in the company. Even though updates do not keep out all pests, they do keep out all known pests. After all, no one wants to fight yesterday's fires. Because of this, it is important to make sure your servers and workstations are up-to-date on their patches. Most computer systems can be configured to update patches at a predetermined time without the aid of the IT department having to update manually every system, everyday. However, it is often necessary to check to see if your machines are doing what they were configured to do.

Operating systems and server software: NT 4, Windows 2000, 2003, Unix, Solaris, Novell, Linux, Microsoft Internet Information Server (IIS), Apache, Microsoft SQL, Oracle, and MySQL.

What you should already know

A Network Administrator's job does not just exist in the server room. Although most Network Administrators should only work on servers, routers, and switches, in reality he or she often spends more time helping the end-users or helping the helpdesk. To become a Network Administrator, you must first know the fundamental basics of server side and client side operating systems and applications, as well as basic hardware issues. Listed below are some of the programs you should already know.

Client Side Programs

- Knowledge of Desktop Operating Systems.
- Client E-mail
- How to connect an ODBC Driver
- Word and Excel
- Backing up user's email and documents

Desktop Operating Systems

A desktop operating system is of course the program that controls the user's PC or workstation. The most common workstation in use is Windows 98, although Windows XP is starting to make some headway. I do not believe that Windows Millennium did very well, as most computer people do nothing but complain about it Because of this; I always draw strange stares when I admit liking it. Even though Windows 98 has not been on the market in years, it is still widely in use in the corporate environment. For security issues, XP Professional far exceeds any of its predecessors. NT workstation used to be the system to use for security but it was with Windows 2000. Some people however, bypassed 2000 and implemented XP Professional as a secure network operating system. I can tell you from first hand experience that it is not. XP's security is too easily by-passed. By simply booting in safe mode, you can gain access to this system.

Even with all of the reported security issues of Windows 2000, it is still the safest bet in a workstation.

*(**Note**: Many software companies may claim that their operating system is secure. The question still remains, secure from whom? A seasoned Network Administrator has the*

experience and tools to access any system he or she sees fits. Today's software companies may speak of security, but what they are really stating is that their system is secure from amateurs, not professionals.)

Linux is slowly making its way to the client desktop, but the system still has interoperability issues in a mixed Microsoft environment. In companies where the IT department builds their own PC clones, you might find Linux as the OS, especially if the Database program is MySQL or Oracle. In the beginning, there was OS2, Geo Windows and Linux. Linux is the only desktop that survived. Linux is still struggling to break into the desktop market. Only those Network Administrators that have been avid loyalist to the program are currently implementing it, but based on Linux's growing trend, it will not be much longer when it will be a stronger competitor to the desktop market.

Connecting Workstations to Network Shares

As with every workstation within a company, you will need to network it to network printers, server shares, and sometimes network fax machines. To achieve this, you should already know how to network a client computer to network resources.

Client E-mail

Outlook, GroupWise, and Lotus Notes are the top three e-mail clients. It is unlikely that you would have access to all three of these programs to learn their configuration menus. Google.com is the computer person's friend. If you are extremely eager and want to try to memorize every program that I mention in this book, you may find all three of these program's configuration tables somewhere on the net. Just type in configuring (program name here)

ODBC Connection

Another important area to know is ODBC connections. ODBC means *Open Database Connectivity*. ODBC is a standard database access method developed by Microsoft. The goal of ODBC is to make it possible to access any data from any application, regardless of which database management system (DBMS) is handling the data. ODBC manages this by inserting a middle layer, called a database driver, between an application and the DBMS. The purpose of this layer is to translate the application's data queries into commands that the DBMS understands. Most accounting programs utilize the ODBC driver to connect between the workstation and the server. Most databases are MS-SQL, Oracle, or MySQL. You must establish a connection between the client program and the server's database with an ODBC link. The ODBC manager is in the Control Panel within Windows 95, 98, Millennium, and NT. In Windows 2000 and XP Professional, you will find it in Administrative Tools. You should easily be able to connect a client to a database using ODBC drivers.

Word and Excel

Microsoft Word and Excel are the two most popular word processor and spreadsheet programs in the world. Many people looking for a higher-end network position often make the mistake of placing Microsoft Office on their resume under computer software knowledge. It is not a mistake to know these two programs, just to place them on your resume, because these are the bare minimum programs that every Network Administrator should know without having to state it.

Backing up e-mail and documents

There is nothing more moving than watching what happens when a mail server crashes and you tell your users that you did not back up their mail because it was just a bunch of junk anyway. Yes, I warn you from experience. It was not that long ago that backup tapes and hard drive space was prime real estate (in other words, it was a lot more expensive than it is now.) In my own arrogance, I did not feel that everyone's personal email warranted the expense of storage space. The server crashes, as they all ultimately do, and I announced that I only backed up the executive's e-mail and no one else's email. A very disjointed, upset mob of accounting clerks, secretaries, and assistants gathered around the server room door waiting with quiet, quivering anticipation, and rope. Completely unaware of what awaited me outside, I was able to regenerate the crashed drive, as it was within a RAID 5. I walked into the hallway, announced that the entire thing was a joke and quickly darted into my office and reworked the back ups.

Server Side Programs

The job description of a Network Administrator may vary from company to company, but below is an outline of what a typical Network Administrator should be able to do:

- Network Security
- User Accounts and File Sharing
- Network Switches / Hubs
- Mail Server
- Internet Server

- Backups and data redundancy
- Supporting the Help Desk and Network Analyst
- SQL Server
- File Servers
- Time Clock Server
- Documentation
- Backups, Backups, and Backups
- Software Licenses
- Monitoring Network Traffic
- Routers and Internet Connectivity
- Internet Security
- Virus Protection
- Anger Management (optional)
- Hardware and Software Inventory
- Ordering computers, parts, and accessories
- Fax Machines
- Print Servers and Printers

I know this seems like a lot to know for your first job, and that is only because it is. Most graduates do not obtain a Network Administrator position right out of school. Without experience, you are more likely to find a position as a Network Analyst, or Help Desk Technician. However, after a year or two of experience, it is possible to find a job with another company as a Network Administrator. Many Network Administrators receive their jobs through battlefield commissions. (The Network Administrator either quits or fired.)

From TheNetworkAdministrator.com...

Frequently Asked Questions About My New Network Administrator.

Many people that have newly purchased a Network Administrator either do not understand them or need advice on how to handle and care for them. Below are frequently asked questions to help you work with your new Network Administrator.

Q: My Network Administrator seems distant and does not want to socialize with the other workers.

A: Network Administrators are private beings that interact best in Internet chat rooms and e-mail rather than on a more personal level. Just give your Network Administrator some time to adjust to his or her new surroundings, and you might just see him or her eventually get to you.

It may also be that your Network Administrator is lonely or exhausted. If after a year, your computer geek still does not fit in with your company try hiring another one.

Q: My Network Administrator constantly insults the other workers.

A: It is never a Network Administrator's intention to insult a co-worker purposely. It is just that there are many times when your Network Administrator is working on several issues at once, (a thing that we like to call multi-tasking), and the section of their brain that is responsible for pleasantries is pre-occupied with running the network, all the servers, the workstations, website, mail servers, SQL server, hubs, switches, routers, and the backing up of mission critical data. When someone interrupts his or her train of thought by asking a stupid question, a Network Administrator responds the best way, he or she can without actually strangling you to death.

Q: My Network Administrator does not seem to have a penis.

A: Ah, do not be concerned. If your Network Administrator does not have a penis, it is most likely that you have purchased a female model. Do not let this alarm you! You can treat her as if she did have a penis. If however, the absence of a Johnson is just too confusing for you, you may order replacement parts or an add-on. However, we do not recommend that you do this, as it will most likely slow down, or even retard your unit.

Q: My Network Administrator does not want to spend his or her days off repairing home computers.

A: Network Administrators are very selfish with their free time, days off and vacations. Many managers do not understand this and they are often confused by the unwillingness of a Network Administrator to repair co-worker's home computers on the weekends. In addition, many company managers confuse salaried employees with slavery employees.

Q: My Network Administrator has access to important company data and e-mail. Should I be concerned that he or she might use this data against my company or me later?

A: This is a common concern with many owners of a Network Administrator. Understand that a Network Administrator is professional, only handles your data, and never looks at it. However, there have been some isolated cases when some Network Administrators have malfunctioned because of being replaced with overseas replacement workers or laid-off due to failing to report correct corporate earners to the government. Moreover, yes it is true that many of these "disgruntled" Network Administrators helped lead government investigators to hidden corporate data. However, this does not mean it will happen to you, providing that you have not been guilty of any of the above actions.

Q: How should I manage my Network Administrator?

A: Network Administrators need little managing. The difficulties with trying to manage a Network Administrator are that most managers know nothing about computers, networks, or well, anything technical. Therefore, to try to manage a person that has a far more superior brain than your own would be insane. Our best advice to you is to let your Network Administrator do his or her job without interfering. Your company will be better for it.

Q: My Network Administrator uses words and a language that I find difficult to understand.

A: The Network Administrator uses a language different from the one you were taught to use in your communications class, liberal arts class, or that MBA. Network Administrators speak in acronyms and only use 0 and 1 in numbers. This is why purchasing a 10K piece of computer equipment does not seem that unreasonable. If you are having trouble understanding your Network Administrator, just ask him or her to explain what they mean. NAs are always willing to explain terms, although, be prepared to feel stupid.

Q: My Network Administrator dresses differently than the other workers.

A: Your Network Administrator has a very good understanding of the importance of corporate appearances. IBM, Ford, and Microsoft have all realized that people work better when they can dress comfortably. Your NA is simply dressing the way that he or she can better perform their duties.

A: My Network Administrator will not address me by my title and does not seem to respect me.

Q: Sadly, you speak the truth; your Network Administrator does not respect you. Many managers believe themselves to be on a higher level than a computer genius. If you cannot correctly program your home VCR to stop flashing 12:00 every time your power goes out, then how can you really expect your Network Administrator to respect you?

Q: My Network Administrator repeatedly touches himself and it makes the other staff members uncomfortable.

A: If your Network Administrator repeatedly touches his or her pleasure centers in public, it could mean that your NA contracted cyber herpes. If this is the case, have it treated immediately. It also falls within Plan B of your company medical benefits.

Q: My Network Administrator eats the other worker's lunches in the company refrigerator.

A: This is a common complaint and one that you should address immediately. Network Administrators that eat out of the company refrigerator can contract dysentery and severe stomach ulcers. If this is happening to you, make sure your NA takes a lunch break either off site or in his or her office behind a shut door without being disturbed.

Q: My Network Administrator is writing a book, reading the news on the Internet, playing computer games, talking to friends on the phone, and building paper machete statues from the magazines of computer parts companies.

A: Do not worry. If your Network Administrator is doing all of this, it is because he or she is happy and considers the workplace their home. Just contribute this to your NA spending more time at work than at home. Many NAs may not even remember that they have a real home. If this type of behavior bothers you, it is recommended that you hire another NA so your current one can go home.

Q: My NA did something good, but I do not know how to reward him or her, so I did nothing.

A: If your NA is constantly doing good things for you and your company, here are a few recommendations to show your appreciation:

- Show him or her some respect
- Compliment your NA from time to time to show you care
- Be a little understanding when your NA works all night, goes home at 8 a.m., and tries to get a little sleep before coming back at noon.
- Money: NA's always view a raise or bonus as a sign you appreciate them.

Q: My NA did something bad, and I want to punish him.

- Thirty years of psychological research has shown that punishing your NA will have severe long-term effects on how and when the government audits your company.
- Do not be afraid to apologize if you are wrong.
- Do not jump to conclusions, because in most cases, you do not know what the hell you are talking about on the subject.
- Do not leave your banking account number or social security number on your computer.
- Do not have an inter-office affair. Your NA will always know. Mostly likely, he is sleeping with her too.

Q: I cannot believe that my Network Administrator is worth what I am paying him or her.

A: Imagine what your company would be like if all your computers suddenly stopped working and no one could perform their daily duties. Ask yourself, how many people depend on their computers and database to do their jobs? Now, how much more would you be willing to pay to make all of that happen again? A lot more, huh?

Q: My Network Administrator makes obscure and meaningless jokes that no one else understands.

A: Ah, this is a tough one. Do not try to understand the humor of a Network Administrator and do not ask them to explain the joke. You have a better chance understanding how hydrogen boils off a star than understanding the humor of a Network Administrator. No, a star like the Sun, not like the movies.

Q: Where do I return my Network Administrator if he or she does not work out?

A: Remember, you do not own a Network Administrator. They perform a necessary function that keeps your company running. If not for the Network Administrator, you would still be using paper ledgers and abacuses.

Network Engineer (Systems Engineer, Network Architect)

Many Network Administrators become frustrated or bored with their position and want to move into a field with more networking equipment and less people. A Network Engineer's primary responsibility is to the company Wide Area Network (WAN). This means that a Network Engineer is in charge of the configuration of routers, bridges, and switches, network planning, analyzing, and throughput. Network Engineers work with the phone company and other network providers. Typically, larger companies employ a Network Engineer on staff.

Education and Certifications

A college degree is usually required for this position, but not necessarily mandatory, as this is a position of experience. However, many companies do require a college degree and unless you are an exceptionally talented computer person, I would recommend earning a degree. **Preferred networking certifications are** Cisco's CCNA, CCNP, or CCIE. Many Network Engineers use Unix and Linux servers to monitor and manage their networks.

Associated Skills

Server and network appliance hardware: Network Engineers work in COLOs, NOCs, and locations that house wide area networking equipment. You will find that most network

Engineers prefer working with Linux and Unix servers for reporting and monitoring networks.

Network configuration: Many large companies have their own private wide area network, and or metropolitan area networks, that connect remote offices to a central location. Frame relay, private T1 lines, fiber, as well as other types of circuits are used. Network Engineers know how to configure routers, bridges, and FRADs to router traffic between these locations.

Routing protocols: Network Engineers work with routing protocols like BGP, IGRP, EIGRP, OSPF, and RIP.

Network monitoring and management: MRTG, is a popular router monitoring software that displays bandwidth utilization over time. Like many other network utilities, MRTG uses the Simple Network Management Protocol (SNMP) to access network devices from which to pull data. As for port monitoring, Ethereal may be the popular protocol analyzer.

Network Security Administrator (Security Specialist, Security Analyst, Security Engineer)

A Security Administrator can be the person in charge of local and wide area network security. He or she can maintain a local or corporate firewall, intrusion detection, security auditing, enforcement, access-lists, IPSec, and anti-virus software. In small to medium-sized companies, the Network Administrator's duties may include security but in larger companies with large networks, a Network Security Specialist can have his or her hands full. Security Administrators are more than just digital security guards; they investigate intrusions, track hackers and virus origins, as well as design and enforce security policies.

Education and Certifications

A college degree is typically required as well as formal training in systems security. Formal training may come from security companies that give classes, certification training, and general experience.

Certifications usually associated with a Network Security Administrator are Cisco Certified Security Professional (CCSP), Cisco Pix Firewall Specialist Certification, Certified Information System Security Professional (CISSP), CompTIA Security+, Check Point Certified Security Administrator (CCSA) and Security Expert (CCSE), as well as the six SANS certifications; GIAC Certified Intrusion Analyst (GCIA), GIAC Security Essentials Certification (GSEC), GIAC Certified Firewall Analyst (GCFW), GICA Certified Unix Security Administrator (GCUX), GIAC Certified Incident

Handler, and GIAC Certified Windows Security Administrator (GCWN).

Associated Skills

Networking: To be a Security Administrator you will need to have expert knowledge in networking, particularly TCP/IP port assignments, packet encapsulation, network topology, and design and theory.

Elements of Security: Security is the largest challenge in computer networking today. A Security Administrator should be well versed on every element of security: Firewalls, data encryption, cryptography, operating system vulnerabilities (OS vulnerabilities have to be kept up with on a daily basis) DMZ topologies, proxy servers, server hardening, strong password conventions, network and protocol scanning, digital certificates, packet filtering, and router security.

Anti-Virus Tools: A virus is more likely to penetrate a network than an attack from hackers. A Security Administrator is also the person in charge of the first line of defense against stopping viruses, trojans, malware, rootkits, and adware infiltrations. A Security Administrator not only should be up to date on digital parasites, but also the software that blocks and removes them.

Network Security Tool Kit: Efficient Security Administrators arm themselves with an assortment of utilities in the fight to keep their networks safe. Here is a short list of the more commonly used programs.

- Trace Route

- Telnet
- SnifferPro
- Ethereal
- Commview
- NSLookup
- NetStat, NBTStat
- Vulnerability Assessments / Penetration Testing
- Nessus
- Microsoft Assessment Tools
- Pstools suite of tools
- Fport
- Tlist
- Kill.exe
- FIRE

Database Administrators (Database Engineer, SQL Administrator, Oracle Administrator, Database Programmer)

Database Administrators (DBAs) designs, manage, configure, program, backup, tune, and monitor the company's database. Because the database is where most companies store their mission critical information, DBAs are responsible for maintaining such important data. Database Administrators work with application developers and report writers to design how information passes into the database. The SQL query language is the programming language used by the DBA to insert, delete, and display data.

Education and Certifications

A college degree is typically required for this position, although a small few have become Database Administrators with experience and certifications alone. Because of the sensitive nature of data management, formal training is necessary.

In this career position, a Database Administrator will need a certification in either Oracle Certified Professional (OCP), or Microsoft Certified Database Administrator (MCDBA). MySQL is also becoming a popular database server program because it is Open Source and works on Windows, Unix, and Linux platforms.

Associated Skills

Server and network knowledge: Because a database is on a server and accessed from a network, it is important for a

Database Administrator to have expert knowledge on at least one platform of server, and desktop to server network connectivity.

Database tools: DBAs use a wide assortment of database utilities in the performance of the job. There are performance-monitoring tools, optimizing utilities, logs, reporting, backups, replication, and distributed transactions.

Report tools: In addition to using SQL queries to run reports, many DBAs use third party report writing software such as, Oracle Reports, Crystal Reports, and Impromptu.

Data warehousing and data mining: A data warehouse is a collection of data gathered and organized for easy analyzing. Data mining is the analysis of data to establish relationships and identify patterns and is typically stored in a data warehouse.

Web publishing: With so much e-commerce and Internet databases, many DBAs create applications between websites and databases. To assist them, DBAs use PHP, ASP, Java, HTML, and XML.

Webmaster (Web Designer, Web Developer, Web Monkey)

Webmasters may install, design, and configure not only the website, but the web services as well. Today's websites are more than just brochures of a company. They use complex scripting, database integration for online shopping carts, and powerful informational search engines. Additionally, websites push down streaming music and videos, blogs, news, and display the largest catalog of books in the world.

A Webmaster is responsible for maintaining, updating, correcting errors, adding new pages and content, and the daily upkeep of the website(s). He or she is also responsible for configuring the web server programs, such as Internet Information Server (IIS) and/ or Apache. These programs, in conjunction with the Domain Naming Server (DNS), are responsible for displaying and distribution of a website.

Web Designers and Developer

Web designers and developers may create the original design of a web site before handing it over to the Webmaster, although in many companies, the two positions are the same.

Education and Certifications

A degree in graphic design or visual arts is a definite plus in the design portion of this position; however, the coding behind a website is what makes it a valuable asset for many corporations. HTML, SQL, PHP, Java, Perl, and ASP are the essential codes that drive web pages on the Internet. Many webmasters compliment their career with such certifications associated with SQL, IIS, Unix, Linux, and Windows.

Associated Skills

Programs: Windows server, Linux, Unix, IIS, Apache, SQL server, Photoshop, Paint Shop Pro, Dreamweaver, FrontPage, Shockwave, Macromedia Flash, FTP, and DNS.

Code: HTML, DHTML, JavaScript, PHP, SQL queries, CGI, XML, ASP, Perl, Image maps, and rollovers.

Search Engines: To increase the hit count on any website, it is important to advertise a website on Internet search engines: Yahoo, Google, Webcrawler, and Lycos are but a few.

Programmers (Software Engineer)

Apart from software companies, larger companies employ computer programmers to write and design company proprietary software. Larger companies with mainframes may have several programmers who are always updating and modifying code to keep up the daily changes of their business needs.

Education and Certifications

Typically, a degree in computer programming from a college or university is required. Nevertheless, I have known self-taught programmers that are doing just fine.

Associated Skills

Languages: C, C++, Visual Basic (VB), Visual C++, Python, Java, Perl, COBOL, Delphi, Fortran, XML, and Microsoft SQL, Oracle SQL.

IT Consultants (Contractors, Temps)

The definition of an IT Consultant is a contract worker who performs a computer related service in a temporary employment capacity "temp." An IT Consultant can be a temporary worker, used for a specific project such as a desktop roll out, or a network expansion. Companies will typically hire contract workers, or "temps" to write, upgrade, or modify code. Many companies like to use contractors because they are highly trained, they do not have to pay them medical and other company benefits and they are easily disposed of when the job is complete. Some companies require their IT staff to start out as a temporary or contract worker for 6 months before hiring them as a permanent employee. This gives an employer the flexibility to dismiss a person that did not meet their expectations.

Being a contract worker is a great place to start if you are beginning a career in information systems. Another advantage to working as a contract worker is higher pay. Contract workers can usually charge a higher hourly rate. A disadvantage in being a contract worker is that once your current assignment is completed, you may experience dead time (time without pay) between jobs. Another disadvantage is that you do not receive the same benefits as a permanent employee "perm." Some temporary companies do offer a medical benefit package, but your monthly payment is much higher than a perm's. Most contract workers at a temporary agency use this position as a way of obtaining employment as a permanent employee. Although some contracts forbid the hiring of temporary employees, most are on a time-specified limit or require the employer to buy out the contract. Some contractors love working as a temporary worker and would not have it any other way. Years ago, I was a Network Administrator for a company in the Seattle area, contracted for a 6-month assignment. I enjoyed the independence of being a contract worker, although at the end of the assignment, I did accept the offer of a permanent position.

Director of Information Technology (IS Director)

The IT Director is the administrative executive of the information technology department. Essentially, this position manages the computer department and is a polyglot (linguist) between the CEO and IT department. He translates technical terms to his bosses and provides presentations. Because this position is primarily a management position, the IT Director can quickly fall behind in current technology because he or she no longer has a hands-on role. Many IT Directors keep up with current computer trends, but rely mostly upon their staff for implementation. The IT Director's primary duties are to provide competent staff, attend meetings, make reports, manage people, and interface with other managers and department heads. Most IT Directors have worked their way up from other positions in the IT department and have expert experience in the field of computers.

Education and Certifications

Because an IT Director is an upper management or executive position, a college degree is often required. IT Directors begin in a lower level computer position and work their way up. In the course of their career, they usually collect technical certifications along the way. Management seminars and classes are helpful in obtaining this position.

Associated Skills

Project Management: Because many large organizations have so many projects at any given time, IT Directors must learn or develop good project management skills. Managing a computer department is like running a business.

Budgets: Most IT departments must adhere to an annual budget. It is often the IT Directors duty to try to stay under budget and they could receive a bonus. Being over budget in an IT department relates to overstaffing, however, in many instances, this is not the case. Poor budgeting from an IT Director often results in layoffs.

Contract and Vendor Negotiations: IT Directors are responsible for contract negotiations. Computer equipment and software is an asset for a corporation that quickly devalues and may need replaced, as company software needs change. IT Directors must negotiate the best price for their company.

Employee Hiring: IT Directors typically have the last word in hiring a new person for the department. The IT Director must play the role as technology expert and human resource person.

Chief Information Officer (CIO)

CIO's typically have no technical background in computers and are either a relative of the CEO or have been selected on their golfing ability to slice a drive on the last hole. CIO's know every secret handshake and are rumored to frequent in the recreation of livestock.

Chapter 3

Looking for a Job

- ❏ What to Expect When Looking for a Job
- ❏ Recruiters, Headhunters, Contractors, and Agencies
- ❏ Working for a Start-up
- ❏ Don't Be Fooled By Job Vultures
- ❏ Discovering Jobs through Word of Mouth
- ❏ Temporary Workers
- ❏ Job Relocation
- ❏ Doing your Homework
- ❏ **Resumes**
- ❏ The Correct Contact Person
- ❏ Writing a Resume
- ❏ Sample Cover Letter
- ❏ Writing Your Resume – *with work experience*
- ❏ Listing Hobbies and Interests on a Resume
- ❏ Sample Resume – *with work experience*
- ❏ Writing Your Resume – *without work experience*
- ❏ Sample Resume – *without work experience*
- ❏ Posting Your Resume
- ❏ When Have You Sent Enough Resumes
- ❏ **The Interview**
- ❏ Interview Attire
- ❏ Cramming for an Interview
- ❏ Arriving on Time
- ❏ Shake Hands Firmly?

- Listening to the Interviewer
- Looking the Interviewer in the Eyes
- Learning from Job Interviews
- Don't Over Answer Questions
- Being Positive
- Negative Image
- When to Talk About Money and Benefits
- 10 Helpful Tips on Lying Your Way through an Interview
- Symptoms Related to Lying During a Job Interview
- Closing the Interview
- After the Interview
- Writing a Thank You Letter
- Worrying about all the Things that can go wrong during an Interview (or *Do-Overs*)
- The Right Fit
- Settling for a Lesser Position

What to Expect When Looking for a Job

Searching for a job is a "job" that most people are not prepared to do. You not only need to train yourself for a career in computers, but also know how to find a job in your field.

Days seem to pass more quickly when you are unemployed, and in a slow job market, you cannot afford to allow even one day to pass without working on finding a job. No matter how many resumes you have sent, you must continually be dedicated to finding a job. Time is against the unemployed and bills do not know the difference in your work status. It is how you look for a job, and what you do when someone does call for an interview, that gives you the edge over your opponents. I cannot say that I am an expert in the field of job stalking, but I have helped a great many people find an IT job, and as a Director of Information Systems, I have interviewed enough people to know what I am looking for in an employee. Perhaps my experiences can help you find a job as well or at least give you one or two suggestions that you may not have considered. In this section, I have compiled some suggestions on looking for work, sending resumes, and the interview process.

Recruiters, Headhunters, Contractors, and Employment Agencies

Recruiters are a lot like a car salesman; their level of professionalism is based on the quality of vehicle they sell. There are good recruiters and questionable ones. A recruiter can be someone that works for a job agency or the company itself. Some corporations are large enough that they have their own recruiters, and it is their job to hire talent. Company owned recruiters often recruit from universities and/ or other companies, however, the most common type of recruiter in the tech industry, works for a contracting agency. These types of recruiters find and place skilled technical workers on a permanent or temporary basis. In many cases, from temp to perm.

Many corporations use temporary staffing companies to avoid paying benefits and taxes. Some companies like the convenience of temporarily employing high tech labor for specific projects and then letting them go afterwards. I once worked for a contracting group on a six-month assignment as a Network Administrator. The money was good; someone from the job agency hand-delivered my check every week, and after six-months, the company hired me permanently. Typically, contract work pays more than a permanent salaried worker does, however you do not receive medical benefits. Although some contracting companies offer some form of medical plan.

There is big money in the high-tech contracting business, and as in any business, there are shady characters. Many contracting agencies treat you like a valued member of their company and offer many benefits; while there are other companies that treat their contractors like cattle. I have heard many horror stories, so it is important to do your research. The best way to research a recruiting or employment agency, is through Internet user groups. If there is ever a forum to voice your opinion, you will find it on a message board on the Internet.

If you lack experience and are looking to break into the exciting field of Information Technology, finding a good recruiting company may be the only way to go about it.

Working for a Start-up

After the *Dot-Bombs,* seasoned IT people are a little more cautious when it comes to taking a job with a start-up company. Too many tech companies sprung up overnight in the 90's, and when they crashed, many people and investment money went with them. Even without the Dot-Bombs of the 90's, you must still choose carefully when considering moving from a company with a stable history to a new start-up company with no history. (*If however, you are new to the computer field or a start-up company is the only job available, then you need to take work where you can get it.*)

It is safe to assume that a company that has made it past its 5-year anniversary has made it past its infancy stage. Although many experts define a start-up company as being in business for ten years or less, which may or may not have achieved profitability in that time span.

There are definite advantages and disadvantages when considering working for a start-up company.

Advantages:	Disadvantages:
• Hiring incentives	• Long hours
• Ground floor opportunity	• Always fire fighting
• Career growth	• Small or lean budget
• Profit Sharing	• Bankruptcy
• Partnerships	• No last paycheck
• Stock Options	• No severance

There are always warning signs when interviewing with a start-up company: excessive talk going IPO and less talk about their products and services. High employee turnover is also a red flag. Employees will often bail from a sinking ship. Adding employees because a company is growing is less of a concern than employees jumping ship. You can always research a company's financial health.

The Securities and Exchange Commission is a good resource to see if a company has filed for an IPO. http://www.sec.gov/edgar/searchedgar/webusers.htm

Better Business Bureau is also a good place to look when researching a prospective employer.
 http://www.bbb.org/

Most computer people will not hesitate when it comes to posting their grievances with a current or former company on the Internet, so use it as a resource when interviewing with any company.

Do not be afraid to ask questions. A healthy company will be happy to answer any concerns you may have about them. Just be tactful. Here are some questions you might want to ask yourself before considering working for a start-up company:

- How long has the company been in business?
- Where is the financing coming from: Venture capital, private investor, from company's own revenues?
- What is the business plan?
- Are stock options offered in lieu of a competitive salary? *When money is tight, some companies will offer high stock options and a lower salary.*
- What happened to the person that previously held the position for which you are interviewing?

Don't Be Fooled By Job Vultures

When looking for a job, it is easy to be tricked by a job ad and show up for what you thought was an interview, only to discover that you are a target for a job scam. Many job vultures lure in their victims by cleverly advertising jobs that do not really exist.

One time I interviewed for a Network Administrator's position under false pretenses. Immediately upon entering a tiny cheaply decorated office, I became suspicious. After a lengthy wait, I went into a small room where a woman with a tattoo on her hand, entered, walked over to a thermostat, adjusted it, and then sat behind a desk in a chair that was much higher than mine was. She lifted my resume with the snake hand and began asking me questions for which she obviously did not know the answers. As the room began heating up, because she raised the heat on the thermostat, I asked,

"Come on, why am I really here?"

She then began telling me the history of her company and the success of their clients. Snake hand brought me in under the false pretense of a job, only to try to sell me a service to make me a stronger interviewer. Their price: $1500.00. If you did not have $1500.00, you could make it in four easy payments, once their service helped you find a job.

I smiled, loosened my tie, and began scolding her for wasting my time and costing me gas when money was tight. Interviewing companies that place false ads are just one type of job vulture. I am sure that there are many more. Whatever your weakness, you can bet there are a hundred vultures hovering to profit from your situation.

I am not saying that there is not a need for interview coaching. I am sure there are people who can greatly benefit from such a service, especially computer people, but a legitimate company is not going to swindle you into their office.

Discovering Jobs through Word of Mouth

There are more jobs to find through word of mouth than listed in the paper. Employers will first call upon their staff to find hires through friends and/ or acquaintances. Talk to your friends, relatives, and former co-workers. Try to network yourself to as many places as you can. Attend events and places where people within your field might go. It is not as difficult as you might think to spot another computer nerd. I have found that computer people are always willing to help another of their kind...providing they are not a threat to their immediate position.

Temporary Workers

Some companies only hire temporary workers, (temps) and then hire them as permanent employees later, if they feel they want to keep them. I was once a temporary network administrator for a company in Seattle for 6-months, after which they hired me as a permanent employee. It was one of the best jobs I ever had.

Job Relocation

Always keep in mind that you might have to relocate to another city when looking for a job. This might not be a pleasant thought, particularly because many people do not want to leave their friends and family and move to an unfamiliar place. However, because of the way businesses are changing, there may be a time that you might have to move away to stay in the type of position you worked so hard to achieve. On the other hand, there are those that cannot wait to move away from their friends and family. I once read where a woman ran into her deceased husband in an airport, 20 years after his death. Apparently, he faked his death. This is probably an example of extreme relocation. To find a job in a slow job market, you have to consider the possibility of moving to another town. *Faking your death is optional.*

Doing Your Homework

The best way to find a job in your field is to research it. Find out what others in your area are doing, and keep up-to-date on technology that might affect your job, making you more desirable to hire. A good way to do this is through the local employment ads. Job listings will let you know what employers in your area expect from you.

Resumes

Correct Contact Person

Sending your resume to the correct contact is an important key to getting an interview. There are those who believe that if you send your resume to anyone in the company, your resume will find its way to the correct person. I know one person who harvested every e-mail address on the company's mail server and sent his resume to everyone in the company. It did get the attention of the IT Manager, but it did not get him a job. What it did do was embarrass the IT department, and subsequently, my friend received a nasty phone call telling him never to contact them again, or there will be consequences. At the time, I thought the shear cleverness from this action would impress them and prove my abilities. It did not, and ultimately I regret doing it.

It is important to send your resume to the person directly responsible for the job for which you are applying. If you send your resume to the wrong person, it does not necessarily mean it will get to the right person. The shotgun effect of delivering your resume, can in most cases, do more harm than good. In addition, never nag a company with weekly or monthly resumes when they are not advertising for a position. It will appear more like spam than a serious interest to work for a company.

Always deliver your resume in the format advertised. Carefully read what the job ad is requiring. If the ad states they want you to send your resume in a specific format, then send it in that format. Most job ads will ask for a resume in a Word document. format, or even just a text format. If you are not sure, send it in a plain text file or inside the e-mail itself to ensure that it will be read. I have received resumes in Word Perfect, Acrobat, Open Office, and a Tiff format, when all I asked for was a resume in plain text.

When clicking through a mountain of resumes, many managers are not going to want to install corresponding software to open your resume.

I have even received e-mails with no resumes attached at all, with a single one-line question:

"How much does the job pay?"
Or
"What type of experience do I need?"
Or even...
"Does a minority have a chance at getting a job here?"

E-mail's with these types of questions without an attached cover letter and resume only make me think the job seekers are not going to pass the company drug test.

Writing your Resume

Cover Letter

It is always a good idea to include a cover letter when sending your resume. A cover letter is a professional introduction to the reader that will tell him or her, the position for which you are applying, and in many cases, it can give a brief foreword to your personality. **Remember**: *You will never get a second chance at a good first impression.* I know that is a cliché, but it is a correct one.

Contact Name

If you can get the contact's name, use it. It is never advisable to begin a cover letter with, *"Dear Sir or Madame"* or *"To Whom it May Concern."* This may show that you are not applying for a specific position, or you know little or nothing about the position for which you are applying. When sending a resume, you should already know the contact name and position. When presenting your resume, you are trying to make an impression that will stand out among many other resumes that are most likely very similar to yours in knowledge and experience. In my opinion, you should spend as much time in preparing your cover letter as you have your resume. A person that would send me a cover letter and resume that is sloppy and poorly put together, does not impress me as a person that can be trusted with mission critical data and computer equipment.

I think my boss puts it best when he says that he hires people to help make his job easier. My boss owns a multi-million dollar corporation that spans across several states. I tell the same to my department; I need people that can make my job easier. I do not want to explain why backups did not occur or simple procedures were not followed correctly.

Tips on Writing a Cover Letter

- Make your cover letter brief.

- Introduce yourself and reference the position for which you are applying

- Present a positive image.

- Never apologize for taking up their time, **but** do thank them for their time

- Always proofread your cover letter and resume. Make sure your cover letter is error free. Remember, a sloppy cover letter riddled with errors makes a statement about your workmanship.

- Focus on the employer's needs and include key words from the ad, like **5 years experience**, or **Network design experience.** Highlight in your cover letter what is relevant to the job ad.

- Try to be original without being corny or too peculiar.

Sample Cover Letter

Your name
Mailing Address
Phone number(s)
E-mail address
(Just one e-mail address will do)

Today's Date

Mr. /Ms. Employer's Name
Title
Company
Address

First Paragraph: "Why you are writing them," This section tells the employer the position for which you are applying. Keep it under 2-3 sentences. Points to cover:

- Why you are writing and the position for which you are applying
- Include where you heard of the position only if it is from a mutual contact or recruiting program. Unless you are told by a recruiting company to refer to them, do not refer to a recruiting company, because in many cases there can be issues there.
- Make some sort of connection, like why you are interested in the position or company. Keep it brief.

Second Paragraph: Explain why you are qualified for this position.

- Give examples of your skills as they relate to the requirements of this position
- Cite **strong** specific examples to back up your claim

82

Closing Paragraph: In another 2-4 sentences, refer to your attached resume. Tell them when you are available for an interview and thank them for their time and considering you for the position.

Sincerely,

Your Signature

Type your name here

In this next section, I separate two different methods in which a resume should be prepared: A resume that can detail work experience, and a resume without work experience. I believe it is important to separate the two, because an employer has different objectives when comparing the two types of resumes.

Writing Your Resume – *with work experience*

A resume is a written abbreviation of your credentials that highlights your accomplishments. You want to impress upon a perspective employer what you have accomplished, as well as what you are capable of doing for them. The format should be brief but have impact. When writing a resume, it is your intention to create an interest that persuades a potential employer to contact you. Many people view writing a resume as arduous as filling out a tax return. It is not - it is worse, but like a tax return, you have to do it.

What a resume is not, is a personal statement about you. It is not a free forum to express your religious convictions or political views, or a biography of your life. I have seen resumes with all of the above and a date of last employment from many years back.

Resume Search Order

When I review a resume for a job that requires experience, I first want to see your current or previous job, how long you held it, and what you accomplished during that time. I want to see your last job first and first job last. Many people will list the first job they ever had at the top of the resume and their most recent jobs on page two or three. You have heard the scary story about the employer only taking 30-seconds to glance at each resume. It is not a story.

I have had 400 resumes on my desk. Being in possession of someone's resume is a huge responsibility to me, which I do not take lightly. I want everyone to have an equal and fair chance on the one job that I have to offer. I must fill some jobs immediately or I have to do them.

Help desk positions usually have a high turnover rate, mostly because the help desk job itself is a complaints department...in a very large department store...that only sells to the insane.

Resumes are sorted by qualified vs. unqualified candidates. In a slow job market, people will send their resume to any ad that contains the word computer in it. Ninety five percent of the resumes received do not qualify for the position. This means that if the employer is not careful, he can sort out qualified candidates with those who are unqualified. This is why it is important to identify in the cover letter your qualifications in relationship to the position offered. No matter how qualified you are for a position, your resume can be easily overlooked, if not prepared properly.

After reviewing the experience of the candidate, the next two things I immediately look for on a resume are certifications and education. Computer certifications and degrees are mounting compliments to experience, and even though experience speaks in larger volumes, a degree or computer certification shows dedication to your chosen career. If a computer job was time served in community service, and there are times when you feel like your job is under a court order, then experience would be just showing up to work. A degree and certification in your field shows that you take your career seriously.

I know it sounds like I am contradicting myself. Both education and experience are very important when pursing a career in computers, and at any given time in one's career, someone is likely to be short on at least one of them.

Listing Hobbies and Interests on a Resume

There are those who will suggest that you include your hobbies and personal interests on your resume as a way to give a little personality to it. I believe this is a big mistake. The purpose of a resume is to influence the employer to select you from hundreds of other candidates. Personal information will prejudge you and it can immediately eliminate your chances of getting the job. In the real world, employers are looking for reasons not to hire you. Placing personal information on a resume in the employer's elimination round is not a good idea. If you put on your resume, <u>Musician,</u> immediately an employer might think that this can be a distraction from your day job, or associate musicians with wild rockers. You never know what some people will associate with your hobby. *Wizard of the ninth order of the chaos dominion* might also be another hobby that can cause a potential employer to question whether you are a good fit in his or her organization. Remember, get the job first and once your probation period is over, then you can wear your Vulcan ears to work.

Sample Resume – *with job experience*

Name
Mailing Address
Phone Number(s)
E-mail Address

Objective:	To contribute my experience and education and provide collaboration to your organization's success.
Objective	*This section is always difficult to write without coming across as a goof ball. I am not sure anyone actually reads it. You may as well write, "To find another job where I can surf EBAY all day." If you do not like my verbiage above, I would search the Internet for samples with which you are more comfortable.*
Experience:	**Jan 1995 – Present** Large Company Inc. Orlando FL<ul><li>Designed Voice-over-IP networks</li><li>Configured Cisco routers / AS400s</li><li>Configured and Deployed network between 30 locations</li></ul>
Experience	*What have you done lately? This is what an IT Manager wants to see first. Put your most outstanding achievements on the top of the page. You can even adjust it to the employer's job requirements.*
Second Job Listed	**Dec 1994 – Jan 1995** List your next job in chronological order.
	State your next job and try not to leave any large gaps between the two. Never volunteer the reason that you left a job. Always make them ask. Some

	interviewers may never ask. Never admit to having been fired. If you must, tell the interviewer that you lost your job to over seas outsourcing.
3rd Job Listed	*I would list as many jobs as you can that are relative to this job position. However, when you get into bag boy and manager of pizza roma, it is not going to help you.*
Education	**Bachelor of Computer Science**, University of California 1982
Certifications	**CCNP** Cisco Certified Network Professional **CCNA** Cisco Certified Network Associate **MCSE** Microsoft Certified Systems Engineer **CCTT** Computer Certified Test Taker...
Education	Under Education, list what degrees you may hold and any honors.
Certifications	Under Certifications, list every certification you have. Some human resource department's screen resumes before passing them on to the IT Manager. Many people might not want to include retired or minor certifications; however, a retired certification might have more value to an employer, because it has age to it.
Computer Skills	List all relevant knowledge that you have, such as, programming skills, product knowledge, past achievements, and any additional computer training classes you may have attended.
Note:	Try to avoid listing word processor and spreadsheet program skills. Unless you are applying for a software support position, most computer managers do not really care that you know how to use Word, PowerPoint, and Excel. You should know these basic programs by default.

Writing Your Resume *– without work experience*

Employers look for different things when hiring for an experienced position vs. a non-experienced position. When reviewing a resume with experience, the first item reviewed is experience - where the person has worked, how long, and what they did. Typically, this information is at the top of the resume. If you do not have any experience, then you must put your best and strongest points in its place. Listed on the next few pages is a sample resume without work experience.

Sample Resume *– without work experience*

Name
Mailing Address
Phone Number(s)
E-mail Address

Objective:	To contribute my training and education and provide collaboration that will help your organization's success.
Objective	*Notice how I replaced the word "experience" with "training." You want to start with this type of brief description.*
Education:	**University of Whatever, 2000** List your Major, Minor, and every computer related class for which you signed up, attended, skipped, and slept through.
Training:	List any computer experience you may have in this section. Part-time jobs, school projects, home labs.
Certifications	**CCNP** Cisco Certified Network Professional **CCNA** Cisco Certified Network Associate

	MCSE Microsoft Certified Systems Engineer CCTT Computer Certified Test Taker…
Certification	The best time to study and sit for a computer certification is when you are attending school. If you are serious about a career in computers, you should get at least one computer certification during every summer vacation.
Computer Skills	List all relevant knowledge that you have, such as, programming skills, product knowledge, past achievements, and any additional computer training classes that you may have attended.

With these objectives in mind, you can easily find enough examples on the Internet to write a clear, decisive, and professional resume. However, if you become frustrated or just do not think you can put together a professional resume, there are resume services that will help you write a good professional resume.

Posting Your Resume

Where can you post your resume so IT managers and recruiters can find it? In addition to responding to employment ads, you should also consider posting your resume in as many online forums that you can find on the Internet.

http://www.Techies.com/
http://www.Monster.com/
http://www.Guru.com/

http://www.Dice.com/
http://www.Computerjobs.com/
http://www.Careerbuilders.com/

These are all great resources for getting your name and resume where potential employers are likely to be looking for staff. When seriously looking for a job, you need all the help you can get.

Network with other computer people as much as possible As I stated in an earlier section, computer departments are more likely to ask for recommendations from their own department first, before placing ads or going to job recruiters. *Someone is always asking me if I know someone.* I have referred and recommended so many people to positions this way. I have even referred people in my own department to positions at other companies when I thought it would be better for them and their careers to leave. If you know enough computer people, someone also knows where there is a job opening.

When Have You Sent Enough Resumes?

Should you send a weekly set amount of resumes to give a prospective employer time to reply? I think if you have to ask this question, and I have heard it asked, you have not been unemployed long enough. In my opinion, you should exhaust every resource and opportunity when looking for a job, sending as many resumes as you possibly can.

It is not enough to send out a handful of resumes, and sit back and wait for a response. I have heard from people in different areas of the country who say that it takes from four to six months to find a job. Can you imagine the stress involved or the bills accumulated in half a year? If I were out of work for six months, I would be asking questions like:

"How many seconds after someone's death should I pounce on his or her former job?"

Information technology jobs are not as abundant as they were in the 1990's, and only those who are the most persistent are going to find one. If you are serious about finding work, you should exhaust every resource. This means that every day you need to think up a new and inventive way of finding a job, and exhaust it.

In my earlier years as a young man, before I became a computer geek, I was a self-employed ceramic tile setter. My father passed this trade down to me. I was self-employed because I was young and no one would hire me. I worked from job to job. This meant that once a job was finished, I immediately had to find another. I lived this way for many years, and during that time, living from job to job did not seem very unusual. Looking back, I do not know how I did it, but looking ahead, I used those same skills to find my first computer job when I had no experience...you can too.

The Interview

Interview Attire

You should try to wear professional attire on a job interview. It is a good idea to have two good outfits when looking for a job: one for the initial interview and another for the follow-up. This is also true if you are meeting with a recruiter for a job agency. A recruiter wants to see how you will represent them when they send you to a client. Although it is true that computer people are usually the most casually dressed workers in the building, (even the janitor wears a uniform) you should dress your best during a job interview. During one interview I had, the interviewer commented on how nicely I was dressed. Because most computer people wear Dockers or jeans, I panicked, thinking he was questioning my credentials. I quickly replied that I bought this suit for job interviews and funerals (I have not been to a funeral in 20 years). He laughed and I actually got the job, but it could have gone the other way, so I advise against such a comment if I were you.

Also, try to avoid tugging at your tie or dress. Most interviewers will notice that you are uncomfortable dressed up, and even though you will not be required to dress like that at work, it is still a negative distraction.

Cramming for an Interview

In many respects, preparing for an IT interview can be like cramming for a test. In order to be prepared, many people will try to fit all they can into their heads the night before an interview. Unless this has worked for you in the past, in my opinion, cramming for a job interview can cause more harm than good. The night before should be used to relax and take your mind off an upcoming interview. There is plenty of time on the drive to your interview to stress out and have a manic episode. If you want to review every computer textbook you own, or at least those areas that you have difficulty remembering, you should do it two nights before the interview.

Arriving on Time

Always arrive on time for a job interview or a few minutes early. *Arriving late for a job interview is never excusable.* I have seen people show up late for an interview, hired, shown up late for work, and then fired, all in their first week. Showing up late for an interview is a clear indication of your work habits. Of course, you can ignore this rule if you are interviewing with your *mother*, someone that owes you a lot of money and your mother.

Just in case, you are not clear on this subject: **Always arrive on time for a job interview.**

If, however, you do arrive late for the interview, and things do happen, simply show the disappointed interviewer your blood-dripping appendage, and explain that you are the only survivor of a horrific accident.

Shake Hands Firmly?

I do not know about the whole "shaking hands firmly" advice when meeting an interviewer. It may have meant something in the early days to test the grip of a potential spear thrower, or catcher in a circus high-wire act, but I do not see any real value in firmly shaking someone's hand. When someone greets me and then proceeds to shake my hand with a firm grip, I tend to want to knee them in the groin.

Listening to the Interviewer

Listen to what the interviewer is saying to you. Some people are so anxious that they do not listen and are only thinking about what they will say next. This might be fine when you are having a conversation with your spouse, but it will not get you far in an interview. Always look alert and interested at all times. You want to follow the interviewer's lead when describing what you do. Bluntly stated, you are looking for "tells," so you can give the interviewer what he or she wants to hear, for you to get the job.

Looking the Interviewer in the Eyes

I used to say that an extroverted computer geek is someone that looks at your shoes when he or she is speaking. Computer people are particularly guilty of not looking people in the eye when they speak. If you are engaged in a conversation with another computer person, it might be fine to stare at your feet when speaking; however, you may have to interview with a non-computer person, or even a Vice President of Technology. Always try to maintain eye contact during the interview...but not too much like you are crazy.

Learning from Job Interviews

A job interview can provide two important functionalities: 1. Providing you with employment, and 2. Experience for your next job interview.

The mistakes made during a job interview are lessons learned for your next interview. However, not all lost jobs are due to mistakes made in an interview. Skill and knowledge are not always the determining factors for hiring; personality and fitting in with a group are factors as well.

In addition, when you are new, and have no real job experience, you can be judged by your learned knowledge, and when tested in an interview, anyone can make mistakes. There will always be questions that you will not be able to answer during an interview. Even an experienced IT person can stumble when being cross-examined by the interviewer. It is an awful feeling not to be able to answer a question during a job interview. In fact, it can be your worse fear, but it can happen.

Instead of beating yourself up, you should immediately write down every question that you felt you did not answer correctly, and study the answer as soon as possible. Once an interview is over, whether you think you did well or not, you should begin preparing yourself for the next one, by using the last interview as an example. If you have to go back to the books, or work it out in your home lab, there is no excuse for answering a question incorrectly twice.

When searching for my first computer job, I must have interviewed with ten or more companies. Each interview prepared me for the next. Every question that I missed or thought I did not respond well, I immediately studied to ensure I answered it correctly the next time. The first computer job I ever held, the interviewer asked me to tell her about TCP/IP. I not only told her about how the protocol is used, but where it is used, and where the bloody thing was invented. With every interview, you gain experience for the next.

Don't Over Answer Questions

People tend to over answer questions during a job interview when they are nervous. Keep your answers direct and to the point. If the interviewer wants you to elaborate, he or she will ask for more information. When asked if you have any questions, do try to ask intelligent questions about the company to show your interest.

Being Positive

Never make disparaging or negative remarks or statements about your current or former employer. Be as positive and as uplifting as you can. Every company has a problem case, so try not to give any indication that it is you. Making comments about fellow or former co-workers might dissuade the interviewer from selecting you for the position.

Negative Image

When I speak of a negative image, I am not referring to photographic film. In fact, in this digital age, I do not even know what that is anymore. *Negative image* refers to the mannerisms you want to avoid when meeting someone for the first time. Lack of interest or enthusiasm can be a negative image. Being overbearing, too aggressive, and acting arrogant are ways to portray a negative image. The inability to express thoughts clearly, and/ or poor grammar and diction can be a negative image.

When to Talk About Money and Benefits

Be careful about bringing up salary, vacations, and benefits too early in the interview process. Let them first bring it up, or wait until you are sure the interviewer is interested in hiring you. When it is time to discuss salary, know what you are worth. Always avoid bringing up your salary expectations first, if you can avoid it. Sometimes you can get the interviewer to volunteer how much a job pays and you can go from there.

10 Helpful Tips on Lying Your Way through an Interview

If truth and experience are hurting your abilities to find gainful employment, and you think you will have to lie to get a job, here are 10 tips to help you:

1. If asked where you see yourself in five years, do not say, "Why, I see myself taking your job, Bob."

2. During the interview, appear laid back, confident, and somewhat arrogant. Kind, meager, and too polite will give you away immediately. An experienced computer person is a slightly bitter one.

3. Do not stare at the interviewer's shoes, groin, or chest.

4. Stereotyping often runs rampant in the corporate environment. Computer people are frequently thought

of as nerds, geeks, and techno-wizards; try to stay as close to that image as possible without seeming socially inept. No one wants to work with a Philbert.

5. You will be judged on how well you can hold up under pressure. If the interviewer begins badgering you about your resume, disregard tip number 3. It may be your only defense.

6. "Self-employed" equals "fired" and may mean you could not find another job. Be careful how you use it.

7. If asked why you are unemployed, blame it on the economy. Your interviewer might show compassion, as he or she may also be afraid of losing their job.

8. If you already have a job and the interviewer asks you why you want to leave, never criticize your current employer. Simply say, "I like where I work, and they like me too, but I am looking for a better opportunity for my family and myself."

9. If asked about your computer certifications, trivialize them by saying that you only got them to put on your resume. Harping about your certification only agitates someone that does not have one and insults those that do.

10. There is always someone in the computer department that is not well liked, and because he or she does not know this, if asked if there is someone like that in your department, answer yes. Because if your answer is no, your interviewer will know that you are the person no one likes.

Symptoms Related to Lying During a Job Interview

There are only two separate instances when lying is an acceptable form of human behavior; while on a date, and during a job interview. Most employers expect you to lie during the first round of interviews. **It is expected of you**. If everyone were judged based on their actual resume, then only overseas workers in India would get IT jobs in America...umm, anyway. If you are going to lie during a job interview, you should at least know some of the symptoms related to nervousness.

- An overwhelming feeling of panic and fear
- Nausea, sweating, muscle tension, and other uncomfortable physical reactions
- Pounding heart or chest pain
- Trembling or shaking
- Shortness of breath or sensation of choking
- Abdominal pain
- Dizziness or lightheadedness
- Feeling unreal or disconnected
- Fear of losing control, "going crazy," or dying
- Numbness
- Chills or hot flashes
- Uncontrollable obsessive thoughts and talking
- An uncontrollable bladder release
- Foaming at the mouth and distemper

Closing the Interview

Do not be discouraged if the interviewer does not offer you the position during the interview. In most cases, they will not. The interviewer may have more candidates to interview before he or she makes a decision. If you get the impression the interview has not gone well, try not to show it. However, if the interview has gone well, I think it is safe to inquire about the next stage of the interview, then money and benefits.

After the Interview

We will keep your resume on record.

I am not sure what "We will keep your resume on record" means exactly, but I would not sit around waiting for them to call you back anytime in the near future. In some cases, it could mean that you are second runner up and if the first pick refuses or declines the offer, you are next in line. Still, I would not get my hopes up.

Writing a Thank You Letter

I have mixed feelings about writing a thank you letter after an interview. I know that every job counselor in the world recommends you send a thank you letter, but to me, the letter is saying; "Remember me. Remember me. Remember me." I cannot speak for every IT Manager, but to me, a thank you note is a little desperate. If I did not already have you in mind for the job, a thank you note is not going to change my mind.

Worrying about all the Things that can go wrong during an Interview (or Do-Overs)

If you were not already worried about any of the considerations that I presented here, I apologize. It is not my intention to make you so self-conscious and so anxiety ridden that all you can do is stare dizzily into the interviewer's eyes, because you are too scared to speak. I am merely trying to strengthen your abilities to gain employment. You may very well experience everything that I have described and more. You will have good interviews and bad ones, and no matter how much you worry before and after an interview, you are just going to have to overcome it. You must continue to push on until you land the job you want (need).

I interviewed a man one time that was so nervous that he looked like he was doing the hot swat sit down dance every time I asked a question. I saw through his nervousness and hired him despite his sitting dance of self-destruction. IT Manager's account for the fact that most people will be nervous during an interview, and unless you just do something extraordinarily peculiar, it is often overlooked.

The Right Fit

With everything else that you need to know in preparing for an interview, what you are not able to prepare for is being "the right fit." It is not enough to have experience, the right education, and handling yourself correctly during the interview, many employers will not select you if they do not think your personality will fit into their group. Whether this is legal, not legal—who knows? This is the fact of life in hiring. What can you do to prevent this from happening to you? You can do nothing about it. If you show absolutely no personality and dry as toast, then you are out of the running for being a dullard.

I do not practice this type of hiring, but I understand it. I have seen computer departments that divided themselves into warring tribes, where the only way to fix it was to fire several people and start again. I have even taken over computer departments where no one got along and everyone was working against each other. I have the personality and experience to put a stop to these types of situations, so I never worry about the right personality for the group. Some managers do worry about it and rely on hiring the right personality.

I have worked with a lot of irritating people. Some so irritating that the mere sound of their voice forced my pleasure centers to shutdown. The worst thing that I have ever done about it is to find them a better paying job somewhere else.

Settling for a Lesser Position

I have met many over-qualified and under-paid computer people sitting on a phone support hotline because they lack, either the confidence or ability, to find a job that utilizes their training and qualifications. It is easy to give up after a long search when there are bills to pay, so you take a job for which you are over-qualified, just to get a paycheck. Nevertheless, what happens with many people, once they accept such a job, they stop looking and might stay for several years in a position that they never really wanted. Several years away from a tech job for which you have trained, will put you in the back of the line. Technology changes too quickly to stay out of it for too long. If you must, take a position below what you want, but continue searching for a job that meets your qualifications. It is like running a long marathon, only to give up 100 feet from the finish line.

Many people have to take jobs for which they are over qualified. This does not mean that you have to keep them forever. Look at Albert Einstein; he was not a patent clerk his entire life. It is better and easier to find a job when you already have one. Always take what is available for now and continuing looking for the job that you want.

Chapter 4

Hack/Anti Hacking Tools and Methods

- ❑ Hack / Anti Hacking Tools
- ❑ First lets start with Windows Registry
- ❑ Finding the Hidden Process
- ❑ Process Killers
- ❑ Network Analyzers
- ❑ Scanning Tools
- ❑ Wireless Scanners
- ❑ Networking Tools for the Professional
- ❑ Vulnerability Assessments / Penetration Testing
- ❑ Microsoft Assessment Tools
- ❑ Command Line Utilities
- ❑ Windows Command
- ❑ Linux Command
- ❑ What to know about Viruses
- ❑ What to know about Security
- ❑ Port Scanners
- ❑ Common Attacks
- ❑ E=mailSpam2
- ❑ Advanced Google Searches (Google Hacking)

Hack / Anti Hacking Tools

Just beneath the upgrade of every new operating system, lies opportunity for the industrious. With every release of new software gives birth to an enormous secondary market of third party products, such as books, certifications, manuals, backup software, utility software, and anti-virus software. This also gives way to new exploits, viruses, and computer hacks. I have read that four new viruses are written per day. One way to view this is that spam, viruses, hackers, and industrial espionage provide employment for some people. A friend of mine believes that "…the worse an operating systems security is, the better it is for our economy, because of the work involved in the daily security of a company's computers. This is why software companies are not held accountable for producing weak and insecure software. Their incompetence stimulates growth." Sadly, I believe there may be some truth in his statement.

As a person charged with the challenges of removing viruses, rootkits, and hackers, you must assemble your own set of utilities to help you ward off intruders. Through the years, I have assembled my own set of software utilities that I have come to rely on everyday. Listed in this chapter are some of the tools that I use.

Hiding in Windows Registry

As with many computer programs, viruses and Trojans must be executed or opened. (In the old days, a line would be added in the autoexec.bat). The first place I always look is in the Windows Registry.

Type Regedit at the command prompt or run box and open Windows Registry. If you look at the example below, Run, RunOnce, RunServices, and RunServicesOnce is where you will often find where a Trojan or virus was opened. You can typically find the virus' location from the execution path.

HKEY_LOCAL_MACHINE
\Software
 \Microsoft
  \Windows
   \CurrentVersion
    \Run
     \RunOnce
      \RunServices
       \RunServicesOnce

HKEY_CURRENT_USER
 \Software
  \Microsoft
   \Windows
    \CurrentVersion
     \Run
     \RunOnce

HKEY_LOCAL_MACHINE
  \System
  \ControlSet001
  \Services\"Virus.exe"

HKEY_LOCAL_ROOT\exefiles\shell\open\command

HKEY_LOCAL_MACHINE\Software\Classes\exefile\
shell\open\command

Also look in the:
- Windows Scheduler and AT command for current scheduled jobs.
- Win.ini(load=Virus.exe or Run=Virus.exe)
- System.ini(Shell=Explorer.exe virus.exe)
- Config.sys

Finding the Hidden Process

Digital parasites and other intrusive software executed on a computer, assign a process number or ID during its execution. Most are in the Windows task manager, but viruses that are more sophisticated hide themselves and require sophisticated software to locate the unwanted pests. These types of tools are enumeration utilities.

Fport – http://www.foundstone.com/

Fport is a great tool that I often use. It reports all open TCP/IP and UDP ports and maps them to the owning application. This is the same information you would see using the 'netstat -an' command, but it also maps those ports to running processes with the PID, process name and path. Fport quickly identifies unknown open ports and their associated applications. Foundstone offers over 30 free networking tools to download from their website.

PsTools – http://www.sysinternals.com/

PsTools is a suite of fantastic and dangerous (in the wrong hands) command line utilities made by Mark Russinovich for Windows. In the right hands (computer professionals), PsTools can automate a computer's shutdown, list a computer's running processes, or kill a process. PsTools is a favorite of network pros and hackers alike.

PsTools include a suite of programs as listed below:

- *PsExec* - execute processes remotely
- *PsFile* - shows files opened remotely
- *PsGetSid* - display the SID of a computer or a user
- *PsKill* - kill processes by name or process ID
- *PsInfo* - list information about a system
- *PsList* - list detailed information about processes
- *PsLoggedOn* - see who is logged on locally and via resource sharing (full source is included)
- *PsLogList* - dumps event log records
- *PsPasswd* - changes account passwords
- *PsService* - view and control services
- *PsShutdown* - shuts down and optionally reboots a computer
- *PsSuspend* - suspends processes

- *PsUptime* - shows you how long a system has been running since its last reboot (PsUptime's functionality has been incorporated into <u>PsInfo</u>)

Tlist – Microsoft Resource Kit

Tlist is a task list viewer found in the Microsoft Resource Kit. This tool displays a list of IDs, names, and windows processes running on the local computer. Tlist is the main tool that I use from my arsenal of anti-hacker tools. It allows me to view not only the processes running on the system, but also locate the program within the server. Once you can isolate the alien program running on your system, you can use kill.exe, another Resource Kit tool, to stop it so you can delete it from your system, or use Pskill.exe to remove it.

Tasklist – Windows XP

Tasklist is an XP utility that displays a list of applications and services with their Process ID (OID) for all tasks running on either a local or a remote computer.

Syntax

tasklist[.exe] [**/s** *computer*] [**/u** *domain\user* [**/p** *password*]] [**/fo** {**TABLE|LIST|CSV**}] [**/nh**] [**/fi** *FilterName* [**/fi** *FilterName2* [...]]] [**/m** [*ModuleName*] | **/svc** | **/v**]

Any one of the previous tools will list every process running in the computer's memory, the name of the program, the directory in which it is located, and a process number. Most digital parasites install themselves on a computer from a vulnerability that is inherent in the operating system itself. An operating system without updated security patches could very well harbor hundreds of viruses, rootkits, and malware. Most are stored in the C:\WINNT\SYSTEM32\ directory. Many are easily identified by their date and unusual names. You must be careful though. If you remove these programs manually, make sure that they do not belong to the operating system.

A command like TLIST –V at the command prompt will display the process ID, the name of the program executed in memory, and the program's location.

Command Line:
C:\PROGRA~1\Grisoft\AVG6\avgserv.exe
 800 cisvc.exe
Command Line: C:\WINNT\system32\cisvc.exe
 860 LLSSRV.EXE
Command Line: C:\WINNT\System32\llssrv.exe
1004 sqlservr.exe
Command Line:
d:\MICROS~1\MSSQL\binn\sqlservr.exe
1016 scvhost.exe
Command Line: c:\winnt\system32\scvhost.exe
1044 regsvc.exe
Command Line: C:\WINNT\system32\regsvc.exe
1056 mstask.exe
Command Line: C:\WINNT\system32\MSTask.exe

Once you have identified the malicious program and its location, you will want to remove it. Sometimes when you try to remove the unwanted program(s) manually, you will often receive an error message that tells you the program is currently in use. To delete the program in question successfully, you must first end the process. I use a program called PSKILL.

PSKILL (process ID)

PsKill

Windows NT/2000 does not come with a command-line 'kill' utility. You can get one in the Windows NT or Win2K Resource Kit, but the kit's utility can only terminate processes on the local computer. *PsKill* is a kill utility that not only does what the Resource Kit's version does, but also can kill processes on remote systems. You do not even have to install a client on the target computer to use *PsKill* to terminate a remote process.

Installation

Copy *PsKill* onto your executable path and type pskill with command-line options defined below.

Usage

Running *PsKill* with a process ID directs it to kill the process of that ID on the local computer. If you specify a process name, *PsKill* will kill all processes that have that name.

usage: pskill [\\computer [-u username] [-p password]]
<process name | process id>

-u   Specifies optional user name for login to remote computer.

-p   Specifies optional password for user name. If you omit this, you will be prompted to enter a hidden password.

process id   Specifies the process ID of the process you want to kill.

process name Specifies the process name of the process or processes you want to kill.

Process enumeration, identification, and deletion are one of the more important skills to know as a computer professional, because it allows you to quickly target and remove unwanted parasites.

Process Killers

Programs, alien or not, run as processes. Sometimes Windows will not allow you to delete a file if it is running as a process, until you stop it first. Here a few programs that you can use to kill a process.

PsKill.exe – From the PsTools suite of utilities.

Kill.exe – This tool is with Window Resource Kit.

TaskKill – Windows XP

TaskKill is an XP utility that allows you to end one or more tasks or processes. Processes can be killed by process ID or image name.

Syntax

taskkill [**/s** *Computer*]   [**/u** *Domain\User*
[**/p** *Password*]]] [**/fi** *FilterName*] [**/pid** *ProcessID*]|[**/im** *ImageN
ame*] [**/f**][**/t**]

Network Analyzers

Network Analyzers / Protocol Analyzers – A protocol
analyzer or sniffer as most people will refer to them, examines
data packets entering and exiting your network. A sniffer can
show you what traffic is dominating your network, from which
computer sources, and if someone is running a port scanner on
any of your systems. Sniffer Pro is a good sniffer program but
it has always been too expensive for me. I like to use two
programs, Ethereal and Commview. Very few computer people
will spend their own money for software, but I did with
Commview, and of course, Ethereal is an open source program.
Most operating systems come with their own packet analyzers,
but they are basic and often clumsy to use. I prefer a real time
program so I can watch the action as it happens.

Commview http://www.tamos.com/products/commview/

CommView is a powerful **network monitor** and **analyzer**
designed for LAN administrators, security professionals,
network programmers, home users…virtually anyone who
wants a full picture of the traffic flowing through a PC or
LAN segment. Loaded with many user-friendly features,
CommView combines performance and flexibility with an
ease of use unmatched in the industry.

Ethereal http://www.ethereal.com/

Ethereal is a powerful multi-platform networker's tool that can be used with Unix and Windows. It allows you to examine data from a live network or from a captured file on disk. You can interactively browse the captured data, viewing summary and detail information for each packet. Ethereal has several powerful features, including a rich display filter language and the ability to view the reconstructed stream of a TCP session.

EtterCap http://ettercap.sourceforge.net/

Ettercap is a network sniffer/interceptor/logger for Ethernet LANs. It supports active and passive dissection of many protocols. Data injection in an established connection and filtering on the fly is also possible, keeping the connection synchronized. Many sniffing modes were implemented to give you a powerful and complete sniffing suite. Plugins are supported. It has the ability to check whether you are in a switched LAN or not, and to use OS fingerprints (active or passive) to let you know the geometry of the LAN.

Snort http://www.snort.org/

Snort is a lightweight network intrusion detection system, capable of performing real-time traffic analysis and packet logging on IP networks. It can perform protocol analysis, content searching/matching, and detects a variety of attacks and probes, such as buffer overflows, stealth port scans, CGI attacks, SMB probes, OS fingerprinting attempts, and much more. Snort uses a flexible rule based language to describe traffic that it should collect or pass, and a modular detection engine. Many people also suggest that the Analysis Console for Intrusion Databases (ACID) be used with Snort.

TCPDump / WinDump
http://www.tcpdump.org/wpcap.html

TCPDump is a network analyzer that displays its results in real time in a Linux / Unix environment. WinDump WinDump is the Windows (Windows 95/98/ME, and under Windows NT/2000/XP.) is similar to TCPDump in that it displays results in real time.

DSniff http://naughty.monkey.org/~dugsong/dsniff/

DSniff is a collection of tools for network auditing and penetration testing. dsniff, filesnarf, mailsnarf, msgsnarf, urlsnarf, and webspy passively monitor a network for interesting data (passwords, e-mail, files, etc.). Arpspoof, dnsspoof, and macof facilitate the interception of network traffic normally unavailable to an attacker (e.g, due to layer-2 switching). sshmitm and webmitm implement active monkey-in-the-middle attacks against redirected SSH and HTTPS sessions by exploiting weak bindings in ad-hoc PKI. ***Dsniff can be a networker's friend or enemy***. I have used it in a wireless network where it captured all the packets from the air of every wireless user without a trace of suspension. Dsniff can be a dangerous set of tools in the wrong hands.

Dsniff:
- Relays and saves SSH traffic redirected by dnsspoof
- Catches SSH access passwords
- Hijacks interactive sessions

Scanning Tools

Nmap http://www.nmap.org

Nmap ("Network Mapper") is a free open source utility for network exploration or security auditing. It was designed to scan large networks rapidly, although it works fine against single hosts. Nmap uses raw IP packets in novel ways to determine what hosts are available on the network, what services (application name and version) those hosts are offering, what operating systems (and OS versions) they are running, what type of packet filters/firewalls are in use, and dozens of other characteristics. Nmap runs on most types of computers and both console and graphical versions are available. Nmap is free software, available with full source code under the terms of the GNU GPL.

Sam Spade www.samspade.org/

Sam Spade is a multi-network query tool with many extra built in utilities, even a tool for spam. It includes utilities such as ping, whois, traceroute, and finger.

NetScanTools Pro

http://www.netscantools.com/nstmain.html

NetScanTools Pro has a Port Scanner, Ping, Traceroute, OS Fingerprinting, NetScanner and custom ICMP packet generator. This tool tests systems and firewalls for vulnerabilities and exposed ports. This utility can also use NetBIOS info to look for open (writeable) Windows shares on the local area network. NetScanTools Pro is an investigation tool that gathers information about the Internet or local LAN users, IP addresses, ports, and many other network functions.

SuperScan http://www.foundstone.com/

SuperScan is a powerful connection-based TCP port scanner, pinger, and hostname resolver. Multithreaded and asynchronous techniques make this program extremely fast and versatile. The Foundstone Group has a multitude of free tools and is a division of McAfee.

NetCat http://netcat.sourceforge.net/

NetCat is a featured networking utility, which reads and writes data across network connections, using the TCP/IP protocol. It is a reliable "back-end" tool that can be used directly, or easily driven by other programs and scripts. At the same time, it is a feature-rich network debugging and exploration tool; since it can create almost any kind of connection, you would need and has several interesting built-in capabilities. This tool is a port sniffer, also.

Wireless Scanners

"Parking lot" hackers are those people that sit in their cars within range of a wireless access-point (or many) and capture free-floating data packets. With a well-configured laptop, a strong battery and a little patience, a parking lot hacker can gain access to almost any wireless network. Even in my own neighborhood, I have logged over 200 unsecured wireless networks within a 2-mile drive. Listed in this section are tools to use against wireless hacker attacks.

Network Stumbler — http://www.stumbler.net/

Network Stumbler is a free Windows 802.11 (wireless) Sniffer. This tool finds open wireless access points, also referred to as "wardriving." They also distribute a WinCE version for PDAs known as Ministumbler. This tool is free but for Windows-only, and its maker does not provide a source code.

Ethereal – http://www.ethereal.com/

Ethereal is an, on-the-fly, scanner that works as well on a wired LAN as it does on a wireless network. Ethereal is a multi-platformed analysis sniffer that is the most widely used analyzer by computer professionals.

AirSnort – http://airsnort.shmoo.com/

AirSnort is an 802.11 WEP encryption cracking tool for local area networks. AirSnort operates by passively monitoring transmissions, computing the encryption key when enough packets have been gathered. AirSnort is a Linux based program that can be installed on a Windows computer, but it is a little tricky to do so.

Dsniff – http://naughty.monkey.org/~dugsong/dsniff/

Dsniff is a suite of programs used in auditing and penetration testing (wired network or wireless). Dsniff, filesnarf, mailsnarf, msgsnarf, urlsnarf and webspy monitors network for interesting data (e-mail, files, and passwords). Arpspoof, dnsspoof, and macof intercept network traffic. All of these tools facilitate the man-in-the middle attack against networks (also known as monkey-in-the middle).

Kismet – http://www.kismetwireless.net/

Kismet is an 802.11-layer2 wireless network detector, sniffer, and intrusion detection system. Kismet will work with any wireless card that supports raw monitoring (rfmon) mode and can sniff 802.11b, 802.11a, and 802.11g traffic.

Networking Tools for the Professional

Ping – The ping utility embedded into the computer's operating system, tests a TCP/IP connection. If you are having connectivity issues, here is a quick tip to follow:

❑ First ping your local loopback address, [ping 127.0.0.1] if you do not get a successful reply, there is a problem with your TCP/IP configuration on the local computer. Un-install and then re-install the TCP/IP Service. If your ping was successful, ping another address on your same network. If you can ping your loopback but not another computer on your network, check your cable connection or see if your subnet mask is correct. If you can successfully ping your loopback, and a computer on the same network, but cannot ping outside of your network, then your default gateway is wrong. Here is a gaggle of ping utilities if you do not like to do it the old-fashioned way.

http://compnetworking.about.com/cs/pingtools/

Trace Route – Use trace route, or tracert in DOS, on a Microsoft computer to help in troubleshooting connectivity issues. Trace route tracks the path of outgoing packets to see which routers they do and do not pass through. Many times a network problem may lie on a remote network and trace route shows you the last successful hop.

Programs like Visual Route, http://visualroute.com/, will give you a graphical view of where your target is and will show you a visual path.

Telnet – Telnet is a utility used to connect to a router or remote computer. Finding a Telnet program that you are comfortable with is important. I liked the one that came with Windows 98 or NT Server. I do not like the telnet program packaged in XP or Windows 2000. I have copied the old telnet program from NT and placed it on my laptop. Hackers typically use telnet to gain access to routers and test open and closed ports.

NSLOOKUP – This program queries a company's DNS server and resolves hostnames, aliases, and mail exchanges. Hackers will sometimes use NSLOOKUP to profile the naming convention of a company. Here is an online tool to help you get the feel for what this utility does. http://www.trulan.com/nslookup.htm

Whois – Whois finds information about an IP address or hostname, including country, state or province, city, name of the network provider, administrator, etc. http://www.whois.net/

Netstat – Netstat is a built in tool with many Windows products, or you may purchase a more elaborate program on the Internet. Netstat displays current connection information and port numbers.

Nbtstat – A Nbtstat command can be used to see who is currently logged onto any Windows system that is still using NetBIOS (all are by default, even Windows 2000). A NBTSTAT -A [IP address] will list the contents of the NetBIOS name table on the target system.

Vulnerability Assessments / Penetration Testing

To test the integrity of your firewall, routers, and servers, a network security company generally performs vulnerability assessments. What they are looking for is un-patched vulnerabilities left open by the Network Administrator because he or she did not install security patches, close port numbers, or secure the system correctly. The last penetration test I ran, I examined over 600 known vulnerabilities. It breached the computer before reaching the third vulnerability. Penetration testing can come in the form of software. Not every Network Administrator has access to penetration testing software, as it is often expensive and typically used by security testing groups. Some companies offer this type of software on a 30-day evaluation. It is worth the effort to search the net to become familiar with the workings of such programs. Below you will find some of the more popular vulnerability programs.

Nessus: http://www.nessus.org/download.html

Microsoft Assessment Tools:
http://www.microsoft.com/technet/treeview/default.asp?url=/te chnet/security/tools/tools.asp

N-Slalker:
http://www.nstalker.com/downloads.php

GFI LANguard:
http://www.webattack.com/Freeware/server/fwserversecurity.s html

Password Recovery

Password recovery should not be confused with hacking a password. A computer professional performs one, while a computer hacker performs the other. (Although is should be said that most hackers are also computer professionals.) There are many reasons why an IT person might need to recover a password; lost and forgotten passwords, corrupt and damaged files, and malicious tampering. There are many "programs" that you can run against your system to expose an unknown password, but most require that you first be logged on with an administrator's account. However, what if you do not know the administrator's password? How do you logon to the system then?

ERD Commander is one of my favorite programs for accessing a computer. You boot from CD-ROM, the program accesses the administrator's account and allows you to change it. ERD commander also allows you to browse the computer's hard drives, obtain network access, and copy files. Admittedly, this program can be "dangerous" in the wrong hands. ERD commander can boot through a SCSI hardware RAID and access almost any Microsoft Windows based program.

ERD Commander
http://www.winternals.com

Passware Kit
http://www.lostpassword.com/

Elcomsoft.com
http://www.elcomsoft.com/prs.html

Command Line Utilities

Command Line Utilities are also important to know. On a Microsoft server, simply type in NET and you will see the following:

NET [ACCOUNTS | COMPUTER | CONFIG | CONTINUE |
FILE | GROUP | HELP | HELPMSG | LOCALGROUP |

NAME | | PAUSE | PRINT | SEND | SESSION | SHARE |
START | STATISTICS | STOP | TIME | USE | USER | VIEW]

NET VIEW, USE, and SHARE are the 3 more useful commands that I use. You can type in "?" behind the command for a more detailed description on how to use this command.

NET USE ?

NET USE [devicename | *] [\\computer\sharename [\volume] [password | *]] [/USER: domainname\]username]

A more useful example might be:

NET USE F: \\servername\C$

You can use a * in the place of F: and it will give you the first available letter and the $ is a hidden administrative share. Often I will access a server from the command prompt by using the hidden administrator share. (Note: so do hackers)

The above is just an example of network command lines used in Microsoft products; Linux, Netware, and Unix have their own.

Windows Commands

The following are a list of command line utilities inside the Windows operating system. Most command line utilities use either /? Or – - help behind the command for usage.

at –command to schedule tasks.

finger – displays user info

ipconfig – displays network adapter info

nbtstat – displays NetBIOS info

net accounts – updates user accounts and modifies passwords.

net computer – adds and deletes computers.

net continue – continues a paused service

net file – lists and closes open shared files

net group – displays, adds, and modifies global domain groups.

net help – displays help for net commands.

net localgroup – displays and modifies local groups.

net name – displays, adds, and deletes messaging names.

net pause – pauses a Windows service.

net print – displays and controls print jobs and printer queues.

net send – sends messages to other computers.

net session – displays and disconnects the sessions between computers.

net share – creates, deletes, or displays shared resources.

net start – starts and lists services.

net stop – stops services.

net time – displays and synchronizes time on computers.

net use – connects and disconnects computer to shared resources.

net view – displays a list of shared resources or computers on a network or domain.

Netstat – displays protocols stats and current TCP/IP connections.

Nslookup – DNS diagnostic and query tools used to look up DNS info on a domain.

Pathping – a router tracing tool that combines the features of the ping utility.

Ping – the Ping utility is used to verify IP connectivity.

Rcp – copies files between computers.

Start – starts a separate window to run a specified program or command.

TFTP – transfers files between computers or routers.

Linux Commands

alias   creates an alias

awk –   finds and replaces text within file(s)

break – exits from a loop

builtin – runs a shell builtin

cal – displays a calendar

case – conditionally performs a command

cat – displays the contents of a file

cd – changes directory

chgrp – changes group ownership

chmod – changes access permissions

chown – changes file owner and group

chroot – runs a command with a different root directory

cksum – prints CRC checksum and byte counts

clear – clears terminal screen

cmp – compares two files

comm – compares two sorted files line by line

command – runs a command - ignoring shell functions

continue – resumes the next iteration of a loop

cp – copies one or more files to another location

cron – Daemon to execute scheduled commands

crontab – schedules a command to run at a later time

csplit – splits a file into context-determined pieces

cut – divides a file into several parts

date – displays or change the date & time

dc – desk calculator

dd – Data Dump - converts and copies a file

declare – declares variables and gives them attributes

df – displays free disk space

diff – displays the differences between two files

diff3 – shows differences among three files

dir – briefly lists directory contents

dircolors – color setup for `ls'

dirname – converts a full pathname to just a path

dirs – displays list of remembered directories

du – estimates file space usage

echo – displays message on screen

ed – a line-oriented text editor (edlin)

egrep – searches file(s) for lines that match an extended expression

eject – ejects CD-ROM

enable – enables and disables builtin shell commands

env – displays, sets, or removes environment variables

eval – evaluates several commands/arguments

exec – executes a command

exit – exits the shell

expand – converts tabs to spaces

export – sets an environment variable

expr – evaluates expressions

factor –prints prime factors

false – does nothing, unsuccessfully

fdformat – low-level format a floppy disk

fdisk – partition table manipulator for Linux

fgrep – searches file(s) for lines that match a fixed string

find – searches for files that meet a desired criteria

fmt –reformats paragraph text

fold – wraps text to fit a specified width.

for – expands *words* and executes *commands*

format – formats disks or tapes

free – displays memory usage

fsck – file system consistency check and repair.

function – define Function Macros

gawk – finds and replaces text within file(s)

getopts – parse positional parameters

grep – searches file(s) for lines that match a given pattern

groups – prints group names a user is in

gzip – compresses or decompresses named file(s)

hash – remember the full pathname of a name argument

head – output the first part of file(s)

history – commands history

hostname – print or set system name

id – print user and group id's

if – conditionally perform a command

import – capture an X server screen and save the image to file

info – help info

install – copy files and set attributes

join – join lines on a common field

kill – stop a process from running

less – display output one screen at a time

let – perform arithmetic on shell variables

ln – make links between files

local – create variables
locate – find files
logname – print current login name
logout – exit a login shell
lpc – line printer control program
lpr – off line print
lprint – print a file
lprintd – abort a print job
lprintq – list the print queue
lprm – remove jobs from the print queue
ls – list information about file(s)
m4 – Macro processor
man – help manual
mkdir – create new folder(s)
mkfifo – make FIFOs (named pipes)
mknod – make block or character special files
more – display output one screen at a time
mount – mount a file system
mtools – manipulate MS-DOS files
mv – move or rename files or directories
nice – set the priority of a command or job
nl – number lines and write files
nohup – run a command immune to hangups
passwd – modify a user password
paste – merge lines of files
pathchk – check file name portability
popd – restore the previous value of the current directory
pr – convert text files for printing
printcap – Printer capability database
printenv – print environment variables
printf – format and print data
ps – process status
pushd – save and then change the current directory
pwd – print working directory

quota – display disk usage and limits

quotacheck – scan a file system for disk usage

ram – ram disk device

rcp – copy files between two machines.

read – read a line from standard input

readonly – mark variables/functions as readonly

remsync – synchronize remote files via email

return – exit a shell function

rm – remove files

rmdir – remove folder(s)

rpm – Remote Package Manager

rsync – remote file copy (Synchronize file trees)

screen – terminal window manager

sdiff – merge two files interactively

sed – Stream Editor

select – accept keyboard input

seq – print numeric sequences

set – manipulate shell variables and functions

shift – shift positional parameters

shopt – Shell Options

shutdown – shutdown or restart linux

sleep – delay for a specified time

sort – sort text files

source – run commands from a file `.'

split – split a file into fixed-size pieces

su – substitute user identity

sum – print a checksum for a file

symlink – make a new name for a file

sync – synchronize data on disk with memory

tac – concatenate and write files in reverse

tail – output the last part of files

tar – Tape ARchiver

tee – redirect output to multiple files

test – evaluate a conditional expression

time – Measure Program Resource Use

times – user and system times

touch – change file timestamps

top – list processes running on the system

traceroute –Trace Route to Host

trap – run a command when a signal is set(bourne)

tr – translate, squeeze, and/or delete characters

true – does nothing, successfully

tsort – topological sort

tty – print filename of terminal on stdin

type – describe a command

ulimit – limit user resources

umask – users file creation mask

umount – unmount a device

unalias – remove an alias

uname – print system information

unexpand – convert spaces to tabs

uniq – uniquify files

units – convert units from one scale to another

unset – remove variable or function names

unshar – unpack shell archive scripts

until – execute commands (until error)

useradd – create new user account

usermod – modify user account

users – list users currently logged in

uuencode –encode a binary file

uudecode – decode a file created by uuencode

v – verbosely list directory contents (`ls -l -b')

vdir – verbosely list directory contents (`ls -l -b')

watch – execute/display a program periodically

wc – print byte, word, and line counts

whereis – report all known instances of a command

which – locates a program file in the user's path.

while – executes commands

who – prints all usernames currently logged in
whoami – prints the current user id and name ('id -un')
xargs – executes utility, passing constructed argument list(s)
yes -- prints a string until interrupted

What to know about viruses

There is much talk in the workplace when it comes to viruses. Viruses are the reason why end-users forget to put paper in their printer and click print 50 more times; viruses are the reason for accidental deletion of documents, and viruses are the reason that many Network Administrators forget to check on backups. Both users and computer people use viruses as an excuse for every problem in a company. Viruses are a Network Administrator's friend and foe: friend because you can blame all unexplained problems on them and foe because they cause you a lot of unnecessary work and your company to lose money. Today's viruses are very well structured and they serve a specific function for their makers. Modern viruses are designed with a purpose that is more organized than simply trying to make a name for its creator. Today's viruses are on a mission to collect as much data as possible. In third world countries where education and resources are not that plentiful, the Internet is an open pipeline. We got it and they want it. "It" is anything they can use, sell, or trade. Just last week I traced a piece of spam that offered a free online mortgage quote to Pakistan. These people were not interested in giving free quotes. They wanted the names, addresses, and social security numbers that you need to provide to get the free quote. This spam was not a virus; however, it still makes my point of what you are up against; viruses are no different when it comes to gathering data. Viruses are interested in obtaining the following information: text documents, spreadsheets, and address books with e-mail addresses, so it can infest itself on to other systems and computers to be used as a mule. (A mule is a system that stores viruses or launches more viruses.) Most viruses today are security problems and you should always be aware of their possible presence. Make sure that WWW.CERT.ORG is in your favorites because this website will help to keep you up on the latest virus and security threats.

Typically, three or four people in every organization send and receive a lot of word documents and spreadsheets, which are often infected with viruses. Spam and personal e-mail are another source of viruses. If you monitor your e-mail as I do, you will find that the vast majority of mail is either personal or spam. Virus makers often embed their creations inside spam that is more likely to be opened. For example, e-mail with jokes, words of spiritual inspiration, and mail warning of viruses that ask you to forward it to your friends, are all designed to trick you into passing it from one recipient to another. These viruses are known as missionary viruses because they travel from place to place with good intention, but carry deadly viruses for your computer. The worst part about a virus for a Network Administrator is to explain how a virus was able to get past you in the first place. Every operating system and network device is vulnerable to viruses. Viruses cause a Network Administrator more headaches than rap music, more aggravation than company executive's home computers, and more frustration than spam. Okay, maybe not spam, but viruses are still pretty darn annoying. Even with virus protection, your system is always susceptible to viruses. (Anti-virus programs only protect a system against known viruses.) Because new viruses crop up everyday, it is easy to forget to check what the latest and greatest threat is and suddenly find that your switch has stopped flashing, or your router is flashing too quickly or a server will not allow anyone to connect. Viruses are more than a nuisance; they are a billion dollar business that is often quite confusing to keep abreast of and maintain. There are viruses that open up computers for other viruses. There are viruses that carry their own e-mail engines so they can propagate themselves with the help of someone's address book. There are viruses that search for text in documents, such as "Confidential, For Your Eyes Only, For Internal Use Only" and then send its findings back to its makers. There are viruses that will cover their tracks by destroying the data on your hard drive or not allow you to install an anti-virus program. To a Network Administrator, a computer virus can be like a cancer that causes you to work late at night, which robs time away from your home and family. Because most Network Administrators work on salary, viruses can cause you to work free.

Computer and Network "Security"

Security is a process of maintaining an acceptable level of risk, and computer operating systems are only as secure as its most recent security update…and new updates created weekly…very weakly. :-) If we compare computer security to the security of an office building, we would have to build a structure with no doors, no windows and no access from the roof. For security reasons, no one could leave or enter our building. Without access to the building, the structure would be useless and might as well be filled with concrete. Therefore, we must open up at least one door so workers can access the building. Now we have an acceptable level of risk. Similarly, if we unplug our server from the network, what remains is a very expensive word processor.

Many companies will throw money at the problem of security with firewalls, intrusion detection devices, outside consultants, honeypots, auditing, forensics tools, anti-virus, and anti-Spam. There are vulnerability testing software and port scanners, Access Control Lists (ACL), TAPS demilitarized zones (DMZ), proxy and packet filtering crypto-capable routers. Once all of the equipment and software is in place, you must watch daily for security updates. The more gears there are in the machine, the more likely the machine will crash. This is the sad fact of network security.

Several years ago, I attended a network security "thing" in Orlando FL. A few minutes before the first session was over, I wandered out into the hallway looking for an adrenal stimulant. (Listening to someone talk about computer security is, not surprisingly, boring.) After filling my free laptop bag with complimentary bottled waters, I turned to discover a spread of computer terminals lining the back wall. I quickly stumbled over where a man wearing a denim blue jean shirt with a logo on the pocket, told me I could use one to check my e-mail. The first thing I noticed was the computers were locked down. The only accessible program was an Internet browser, not Internet Explorer or Netscape, but Mozilla. Within seconds, I discovered the ability to open telnet and used it to check my e-mail. I closed it, turned around as the meeting was ending, and began to walk away with a pleased smile on my face. Later that day, someone told me the computers were placed there to show off the company's security talents. There was one flaw in their set up, it was the telnet program, and more than half the people attending the conference discovered it.

Because there is no such thing as total security, this does not necessarily mean that you can give up. You must make a concerted effort to keep out the amateur hackers. In this next section, I explain basic tools used for network security.

Firewalls

Typically, a firewall will sit as a sentry between your network and the rest of the world. Firewalls will analyze data packets and compare requests against a pre-configured security list. Many Network Administrators configure their routers with security access-lists to avoid the necessity of a Firewall. Firewalls can also slow access speeds because it inspects every packet.

Cisco Pix Firewalls – Cisco Pix firewalls are a security appliance with a built in operating system. Pix firewalls are a valued instrument to know and have on your resume. **642-521 CSPFA** Exam number 642-521

Checkpoint – One of the most popular software based firewalls.

NetScreen – An excellent hardware based firewall that keeps your traffic moving at line speed.

Symantec Firewall/VPN – An integrated security and networking device that provides easy, secure, and cost-effective Internet connectivity between locations.

Fortinet – Dedicated hardware/software platforms that break the Content Processing Barrier, supporting network-based deployment of application-level services - including virus protection and full-scan content filtering - and enabling organizations to improve security, reduce network misuse and abuse, and better utilize their communications resources, without compromising network performance.

Zone Alarm – Provides solid, basic PC protection for the home user. Zone Alarm is an intuitive user interface that makes firewall management easier than ever, as well as a host of security enhancements. Zone Alarm is free for personal use. It is excellent for VPN users, too.

Virtual Private Networks (VPN) – Virtual private networks provide an encrypted connection between a user's distributed site over a public network (e.g., the Internet). By contrast, a private network uses dedicated circuits and encryption. The basic idea is to provide an encrypted IP tunnel through the Internet that permits distributed sites to communicate securely. The encrypted tunnel provides a secure path for network applications and requires no changes to the application.

Proxy Servers – This server sits between a client application, such as a Web browser, and a real server. It intercepts all requests to the real server to see if it can fulfill the requests. If not, it forwards the request to the real server.

Linux servers have a great built-in proxy program. Here is a good link on the net that does a good job explaining how to configure a proxy server using Linux.
http://www.tldp.org/HOWTO/Firewall-HOWTO.html

Wingate is popular proxy software for Windows.
http://www.wingate.com/

Access Lists – An access list is generally associated with a router or a computer that is acting as a Firewall. Simply put, an access list either accepts or rejects access to network resources as configured in its tables. A Cisco router utilizes access list as a security measure to either route traffic to its intended destination or reject it by sending it to a bit bucket (a null port configured to route a packet to nowhere instead of wasting resources by rejecting it to its originator).

Demilitarized Zone (DMZ) – **DMZ** is a computer or small sub-network that sits between a trusted internal network, such as a corporate private Local Area Network, and an untrustworthy external network, such as the public Internet. Typically, the DMZ contains devices accessible to Internet traffic, such as Web (HTTP) servers, FTP servers, SMTP (e-mail) servers, and DNS servers. The term comes from military use, meaning a buffer area between two enemies.

Honeypots & Tar Pits – An Internet attached server that acts as a decoy, luring in potential hackers in order to study their activities and monitor how they are able to break into a system.

Honeypots are designed to mimic systems and limit the intruder from having access to an entire network. If a honeypot is successful, the intruder will have no idea that she or he is being tricked and monitored. Most honeypots are installed inside a firewall so they can better be controlled, though it is possible to install them outside firewalls. A honeypot in a firewall works in the opposite way that a normal firewall works: instead of restricting what comes into a system from the Internet, the honeypot firewall allows all traffic to come in from the Internet and restricts what the system sends back out. If you want to learn more about "Honeypots" or "How to Create a Honeypot," follow the links below.

http://www.spitzner.net/honeypots.html

http://www.auditmypc.com/freescan/readingroom/honeypot.asp

Auditing – Event auditing logs either equipment or security actions such as deleted files, failed logons, and sometimes unauthorized tampering. Event auditing can be used to prevent security break-ins or forensics work after the fact, when it is too late.

Common Attacks

Attacks against IP are the most common method of penetrating a node because it is the network protocol of the Internet. For any type of computer equipment to participate on the Internet, it requires a valid IP address and a hardware address. The network card manufacturer burns a hardware address on every network card. This number is unique to every other network and expressed in a hexadecimal value. An IP address is also unique and assigned either statically or dynamically by your Internet provider. An IP address can be tracked to its origination point where it enters the Internet. This is where many hackers use some form of IP Spoofing. IP Spoofing is someone purposely uses a forged IP address so their exploits cannot be tracked to their computer or location. IP and ARP (hardware addresses) are commonly spoofed, although these days, I do not know how effective it is.

Denial-of-Service – On the Internet, a denial of service (DoS) attack is an incident in which a user or organization is deprived of the services of a resource they would normally expect to have. Typically, the loss of service is the inability of a particular network service, such as e-mail, to be available or the temporary loss of all network connectivity and services. For example, a Web site accessed by millions of people is forced to cease operation temporarily. A denial of service attack can also destroy programming and files in a computer system. Although usually intentional and malicious, a denial of service attack can sometimes happen accidentally. A denial of service attack is a type of security breach to a computer system that does not usually result in the theft of information or other security loss. However, these attacks can cost the target person or company a great deal of time and money.

Buffer Overflows – A buffer overflow occurs when a program or process tries to store more data in a buffer (temporary data storage area) than it is able to hold. Since buffers can only hold a specific amount of data, the extra information—that has to go somewhere—can overflow into the adjacent buffers, corrupting or overwriting the valid data stored. In buffer overflow attacks, the extra data may contain codes designed to trigger specific actions, in effect, sending new instructions to the attacked computer that could, for example, damage the user's files, change data, or disclose confidential information.

Data Diddling – This kind of an attack involves altering the raw data just before a computer processes it and then changing it back after the processing has completed.

E-mail Spoofing – A spoofed e-mail is one that appears to originate from one source but is actually from another source.

Mail Spamming – Spammers utilize this type of spoofing from mail servers that allow open forwarding. Because most companies do not employ an E-mail Administrator, most Network Administrators do not know to close this vulnerability.

Worm / Virus Attack – This form of Virus is a program that attaches to a computer or a file and then propagates to other files and computers on a network.

Logic Bombs – This is an event-dependent program that relies on a specific event, such as a date, to trigger the execution of the virus. (For example, the Chernobyl virus).

Password Cracking – Password cracking is not as complex a procedure, as many people would think. I can tell you from experience that more than half of all passwords within a company are identical to any other company. People, as well as Network Administrators, tend to use the same passwords. Most of the time, password cracking is more like password guessing. A network is only as secure as its passwords. Passwords are an ineffective security measure. They do not keep out the internal or external hackers, pranksters, and criminals (there is software that can guess half of the passwords in an average organization in only a couple of hours); Passwords are an administrator's nightmare. Users are constantly forgetting their password, even though it is typically their child or pet's name. Many Network Administrators force password expirations. This means they have configured the server to force the user's passwords to expire so they must change to a new password as a means of security. In my opinion, this practice causes more work for the Network Administrator than it does protecting the network.

Confidentiality Breaches – It has been reported that ninety percent of all security breaches are from the inside the company by employees. It is common to monitor e-mail to help protect a company from lawsuits or from valuable information being sent outside the company. I have seen everything you could possibly imagine from monitoring e-mail, such as pictures of hairy babies, adultery, and embezzlement. For this reason, most corporations monitor e-mail and if this surprises you, it is only because you have not been careful yourself. Every packet of data that leaves and enters your router is more than likely being monitored from either within your company or from outside entities.

E=mailSpam2

E-mail has done for communication what the Internet has done for pornography; *there is more than the mind can ever comfortably comprehend.* Spam has played a particularly large role in propagating both. There is no question that spam is an annoyance. Within Spam are unwanted advertisements such as, diet pills, home refinancing, sexual aids, and porn sites. There is virus spam, phishing spam (phishing is a pop name for identity stealing), and there is spam that is used to do nothing more then cause a buffer overflow on the mail server so it can send more spam.

Spammers do not use their own e-mail servers to send spam. They exploit a method called **Open Relay** on unsecured e-mail servers.

Open Relay Exploit

Open relay is when an e-mail server allows third-party e-mail messages to relay. (Many times, it is open by default.) By allowing your mail server to relay mail, your server is vulnerable to use by spammers to relay large volumes of spam mail to their targets. If your server allows third-party mail to relay, your company can be subject to Internet block lists, and even in some cases, legal damages caused by the negligence of not securing your mail server. (Even though the software maker has set this as a default setting) To test if your mail server can relay mail, or if your company's domain is on a boycott list, you can go to http://www.ordb.org/ and have your server tested. You may also test it yourself by following these instructions.

Step 1.
Use telnet on port 25 to telnet into your server:
(Remember to configure your telnet program for "echo;" otherwise, you will not be able to see what you are typing. Also, typos will error out your task and you will have to reset the session.)

telnet (server IP Address) 25

220 servername.domain.com Microsoft ESMTP MAIL Service, Version: 5.0.2195.6713 ready at Tue, 3 May 2005 10:57:49 -0400

> ehlo

250-mailserver.domain.com Hello [192.168.1.1]
250-TURN
250-ATRN
250-SIZE 4194304
250-ETRN
250-PIPELINING
250-DSN
250-ENHANCEDSTATUSCODES
250-8bitmime
250-BINARYMIME
250-CHUNKING
250-VRFY
250-X-EXPS GSSAPI NTLM LOGIN
250-X-EXPS=LOGIN
250-AUTH GSSAPI NTLM LOGIN
250-AUTH=LOGIN
250-X-LINK2STATE
250-XEXCH50
250 OK

>mail from:testingmailserver@test.com

250 2.1.0 testingmailserver@test.com....Sender OK

> rcpt to:testaccount@yahoo.com
550 5.7.1 Unable to relay for testaccount@yahoo.com

550 5.7.1 Unable to relay for testaccount@yahoo.com
is the response for a properly configured mail server with a
secured open relay. If relaying were open, then you would
receive the following response.

250 2.1.5 testaccount@yahoo

250 means OK.
For more information on "open relay," refer to your favorite
Internet search engine.

Buffer Overflow Spam

Some mail servers are vulnerable to "buffer overflows." A
spammer can target a mail server with thousands of random
names @yourDomain.com. When the mail server replies that,
there is no user name at that domain, and because of the shear
volume of rejections, a buffer programmed to handle this
request is "overflowed," resulting in allowing spam to pass.

Advanced Google Searches
(Google Hacking)

Google is such a powerful search engine, that hackers use it to find passwords and confidential or sensitive documents that companies do not realize are available to the public. Most computer people use Google, but do not know how to use all of its search parameters. The term "Google hacking" is a method used by unscrupulous people to uncover sensitive data, as well as expose web server vulnerabilities. Listed below are several Google search parameters and examples.

filetype:

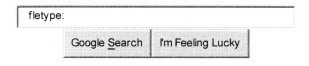

The syntax "filetype:" instructs Google to search for files on the Internet with specific extensions. For example: **filetype:doc site:gov confidential** Google will produce all the word documents, from all the gov domains that may contain the word confidential. Another example is, **filetype:pdf site:com access-list**. You may use any domain type, (com, gov, edu…)

cache:

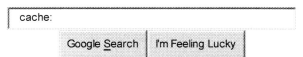

The syntax "**cache:**" will display the version of the web page that Google has in its cache. For example:

"cache:www.microsoft.com" will display Google's cache of the Microsoft homepage.

intext:

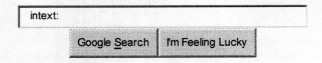

The syntax "**intext**" searches for the words within a specific website and ignores the URLs and page titles. For example: **intext:confidential** will return only links to those web pages that have the search keyword " **confidential** " in its webpage.

intitle:

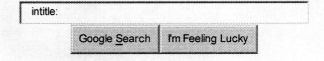

The syntax "intitle:" instructs Google to search for pages that contain the words behind intitle: For example intitle:index of master.passwd will return pages within Unix or Linux where the master.passwd files are. /etc/passwd "allintitle:" will produce a list of all words in the title. Google will ignore the slashes.

intitle: examples:

intitle:"Index of" .sh_history

intitle:"Index of" .bash_history
intitle:"index of" passwd
intitle:"index of" people.lst
intitle:"index of" pwd.db
intitle:"index of" etc/shadow
intitle:"index of" spwd
intitle:"index of" master.passwd
intitle:"index of" htpasswd
intitle:"index of" members OR accounts
intitle:"index of" user_carts OR user_cart
allintitle: sensitive filetype:doc
allintitle: restricted filetype :mail
allintitle: restricted filetype:doc site:gov

inurl:

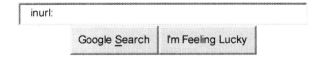

The syntax "**inurl:**" instructs Google to search for pages that contain specific words or characters included in the URL such as this **inurl:windows**. The results of this query will produce such pages that have the word "windows" in it. **allinurl:** will produces the results of URLs with all of the specified words in its query. **allinurl:windows/cracks**.

inurl: examples:

inurl:admin filetype:txt
inurl:admin filetype:db
inurl:admin filetype:cfg
inurl:mysql filetype:cfg
inurl:passwd filetype:txt
inurl:iisadmin
inurl:auth_user_file.txt
inurl:orders.txt
inurl:"wwwroot/*."
inurl:adpassword.txt
inurl:webeditor.php
inurl:file_upload.php
inurl:gov filetype:xls "restricted"

link:

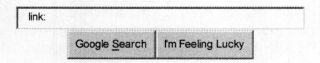

The syntax "**link:**" will produce a list of webpages that have a link to a specified webpage. For example: **link:www.thenetworkadministrator.com** will create a Google list of websites with links to www.thenetworkadministrator.com.

phonebook:

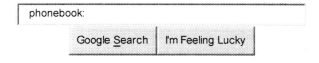

The Google syntax **"phonebook"** searches for U.S. street addresses and phone number information. For Example: "phonebook:James+FL" will list all names of persons having "James" in their names and located in "Florida (FL)."

related:

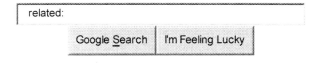

The syntax **related:** lists web pages that are "similar" to a specific web page. For Example: **related:www.thenetworkadministrator.com** will list web pages that are similar to that of TheNetworkAdministrator's homepage.

site:

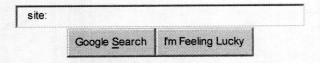

The syntax **site:** instructs Google to search for keywords in a particular site or domain. For example: **exchange site:microsoft.com** will search for the keywords "exchange" in those web pages in all the links of the domain microsoft.com.

Chapter 5

Managing Your Network and Server Room

❑ Learning Under Fire or Submersion Learning
❑ Know The Server Room
❑ Know Your Servers
❑ Rebooting a Server
❑ Passwords
❑ What Server Operating Systems Should I Know
❑ What To Do When a Server Crashes
❑ The Recommended Back Up Strategies
❑ Troubleshooting Tips:
❑ Upgrades

Learning Under Fire or Submersion Learning

One of the very first things some new computer people must come to grips with when he or she takes over a position is that the **person who preceded you did not leave behind any software or documentation**.

Most computer people do not take the time to document the details of the job and instead, keep information about their job duties stored safely in their heads.

> **Notation:**
> *This in not typically true of programmers: Programmers are trained to document their work and add comments in their code to help future programmers.*

There has been much speculation as to why this occurs: (mostly by me) job security, laziness, or perhaps in many cases, there was just not enough time.

A friend of mine, Michael, called me one morning and told me that his company was bought out and the new management asked him to document his duties and all the servers he maintained. He asked what I thought of the request. My thoughts on this were obvious; he was just about to lose his job. My advice was to spend his time looking for a new job and it was up to him whether he wanted to make it easier for his replacement. He chose to look for a new job and just in time too. His revenge was short-lived as a friend of his replaced him. It was a great opportunity for his friend and Michael could not refuse his friend's request for help. It is irresponsible and unprofessional for a computer person not to document his or her duties. Then again, how responsible do you want to be to a company that is about to fire you?

The systems and equipment stored in a server room is the core of a modern business, and it is the least documented. I have built server rooms from scratch and taken over existing ones. Neither one seems more difficult than the other does. The disadvantage of taking over an existing server room is learning the personalities and eccentricities of older servers. Each server has its use, its own set of unique programs, and its own quirks. Most can be fixed with as little as a reboot, or an occasional driver reinstall. If you know each computer's quirks, you are the master of your company's data core. If however, you are new to the company, and have never actually managed a server room before, a down database server in a large company can be brown trousers time.

I have taken three senior IT positions where there was no software or documentation. With all of the emotions associated with being a new IT person, such as the fear of being exposed as inexperienced, possible rejection from your peers and being fired for gross incompetence, having to explore the server room without a road map is not going to make your first couple of weeks easier. So what do you do?

Let us say you are a new Network Administrator, holding the position for the first time, and you open the server room door and see a waterfall of blue cable crashing into what looks like a stack of hubs—you think—or they could very well be switches, which they probably are. You turn to see a motley crew of misshaped servers, more cables turned and twisted around metal racks bridged by what looks like a jungle gym in the monkey cage. Do not panic yet!

I know of a person that after the second day on the job, he left a note on his boss' desk admitting to her that he did not know what he was doing and that his brother was the one on the phone for the technical interview. (I am not making this up) He thought he could fake his way through the job until he could learn, but the server room frightened him and he panicked. The story does not end there. Even though he lied, the company still called him and asked him to come back. He worked there another two years before getting a better job with a larger company. One of the best things about working in IT is you have access to expensive equipment and **you are being paid to train yourself for your next better paying job**.

The fellow in my story got lucky. It is unusual that a company would actually invite you back. The thing he should have realized is that in a situation like his, where there were no other computer people, he could have easily faked his way until he learned. He could have called his brother, or gave his brother remote access until he learned the systems. <u>Because</u>, the simple fact is, no one knows what computer people do and they are afraid to ask because they do not want to look stupid when they do not understand you. It is just like when you try to explain a computer thing to a family member. They just gawk at you as if you are speaking in another tongue.

Our friend in the story collapsed too quickly. He had too many resources available to him to quit. He had his brother, the Internet, and software support. He almost lost one of the best opportunities available in this business. Learning under fire is an accelerated level of education that you cannot get anywhere else. You learn faster, with more retention, and more clarity, providing you do not have a nervous breakdown. Your aim is always to find jobs that you are under-qualified for, not over-qualified. If you take a job for which you are over-qualified, you will be bored and hate it. Computer people must have a challenging job, or it is straight to EBay and the porn sites.

If you are ever in a situation for which you feel you are vastly under-qualified, approach it with confidence and cool control. If you appear confident, no one will question you. Do not volunteer anything that you do not have to, and when someone asks you a question you cannot answer, just look at him or her as if he or she is an idiot until you can answer it. Confidence and leadership is a great substitute for experience. These same traits elect presidents and they will work well in the IT department too.

Know the Server Room

To the untrained eye, a server room is a brilliant futuristic display of blinking lights, panels with a mish mash of wires and cables looping in and out of seemingly bizarre looking equipment and all doing so in a very mysterious manner. To the trained eye, he or she might see an entanglement of patch cables and power cords that would take a hook knife to disentangle, and servers that are too old to use and too heavy to move. Server rooms are cool, alive with the sound of fans buzzing, power supplies humming and in the dark with diodes blinking like stars in the nighttime sky. To a computer geek, a server room is a wondrous place. However, it can also be a scary place if it is your job to take care of it and you do not know what to do. If you have never been in a server room before, it can be quite an intimidating experience. Remember, what Douglas Adams said, "**Don't panic.**" I am here to help you untangle the cables and tell you where they are going.

I think the best place to start is at the top and work your way down. At the top is the router and demarc.

The **demarc** is the line of demarcation, where the phone company's responsibility ends and yours begins. Typically, this might be with the patch cable coming from the CO's (phone company) equipment such as a smart jack. This device terminates a T1 line or other type of data circuit. Your responsibility begins with the cable between the CSU/DSU and the smart jack, or demarc. The smart jack is a rather small metal box, mounted sideways against the wall with a phone company sticker and circuit ID numbers written on it. It can also be a small cabinet with server circuits. From this device, you will find a network cable plugged into your company's CSU/DSU.

The **CSU/DSU** is a device that multiplexes and de-multiplexes the signal and separates the channels coming from the smart jack. (In other words, the data stream coming from the Internet to your network.) These days, the CSU/DSU is built into the router, but in older systems, and there are still many of them out there, the CSU/DSU can be a separate unit that is connected to the smart jack by a CAT 5 patch cable and attached to the router using a specified cable by the router maker. From the CSU/DSU the next connection is to the router.

Router – Like the name suggests, a router "routes" data packets from source to destination and from destination to source. A router can also be used as a firewall to pass packets or block them. Cisco, Bay Networks, and Adtran are some brand names to be familiar with, Cisco being the largest and most well known. From here, the router passes its data either to a switch, hub, or even a firewall. I will discuss all three.

Firewalls – A firewall may be a barrier between the router and switch (or hub). The basic physical design of a firewall is a computer or hardware box that has multi-honed network cards, or multiple network cards. The router and patch cable may connect to one of the firewall's network cards and from there it is routed out to an out-going network card to either the internal network or the network that contains your web machines. A network is nothing more than the hub or switch that is connected to your computers. Firewalls are programmed to allow desired traffic in and undesired traffic out.

A Hub – A hub is the most basic of networking devices that are rapidly being replaced with switches as switch prices have come down. A typical hub might have 24 ports, (24 slots for patch cables with RJ-45 end connectors). A hub acts as a crossover cabling allowing all computers connected to it to communicate with each other. Hubs are slow. They allow broadcast to every computer on the network instead of just the one for which the packet is intended, and are typically to blame for most network bottlenecks.

Switches – In appearance, a switch looks very similar to a hub. The main difference is that a switch knows the hardware and sometimes IP address of every computer connected to it and will pass data to only the intended recipient and not the entire network like a hub does. Switches are faster, more reliable and hold a network table of every node connected to it.

Patch Panel – A patch panel is nothing more than a wiring block. It is a place where all cables merge from the entire networking wall jacks in an office. The networking cable of eight wires or four pairs is punched down to the patch panel with a punch down or impact tool. The other end of the cable, the computer side, is punched down to a wall jack. There are patch panels for category 4, 5, and 6 cables and also category 3 phone cables and fiber optic cables. The connection ends from the wall jack to your computer.

Now let us do it backwards:
From your **computer** and network, patch cable plugs into a **wall jack** that is connected to a cable that is punched down to a **patch panel**. From the patch panel and network, cable is plugged into a **switch** or **hub**, from there a cable is plugged into a **firewall** or **router**, to the phone company's **smart jack**, otherwise known as the line of **demarcation**.

Computer → Wall Jack → Patch Panel → Hub or Switch → Firewall or Router → Smart Jack or Demarc

UPS

Of course, the server room would not be complete without a UPS, (**Uninterrupted Power Supply**) A UPS is what all the equipment above is plugged into. In the event of a power surge or temporary power outage, a UPS can be configured to shut down your servers safely if the outage is too long and it will warn your users. A UPS can be rack-mounted or be as large as a washing machine. It is the device that all of the other devices plug into.

Know Your Servers

Taking charge of an unknown server room can sometimes be an overwhelming task. Servers can be stacked like unlabeled boxes in a warehouse, with no discernable pattern of intent. In other words, you will not know what each server does, unless you know how to look. At least one time, in every computer administrator's career, he or she will have to enter a server room and begin the arduous task of trying to differentiate what each server does.

With a little help from me, and a small notebook, walk into the server room and click to life each server and document which server does what, their names, and IP addresses. What I like to do is change the background on the desktop by typing in the name of the server.

If you are just taking over a server room, here are some tips to help you identify the important machines that you should note.

Database Servers

Isolate which servers are the database servers, as these are your company's most valued systems. Database servers store all the company's important data. Write down their names, IP addresses, and record any ODBC connections in the ODBC manager. (ODBC Manager is in the Control Panel on a Microsoft system. Otherwise, your company uses Oracle). Immediately following the discovery of the database servers, check how they are backed up and then locate the backups. In a well-configured database environment, there should be at least two identical database servers, the actual working server and a redundant backup for testing or running reports. It is not likely that you would be expected to administer the company's database servers unless you already had expertise in this area. You will however, be responsible for backups.

File and Print Servers

There are always file and print servers inside a company's server room. These machines exist to store all the personal files for each department so they can be safely backed up at night. Record all server shares to your notepad so you can reference them quickly, as you will most likely have to solve a printer-related problem straight away or restore an accidentally deleted file. Record the file and print servers name, the IP address, and all the print shares. These servers are usually low on memory and need upgraded. Printers are the number one reason that computer professionals consider joining Green Peace. If ever there were a perpetual motion of wasted energy, it would be how often office workers print out documents, review them, and then promptly put them through the shredder. Once a week, I have seen an office supply courier carting in a load of printing paper, then six days later I have seen someone else carrying out giant balls of shredded paper to the dumpster. If during a job interview you receive an odd question about printers, the best response is to shiver and look grim. Most likely, it was a question to test your experience level. An experienced computer person is one that has been affected by printers.

Time Clock Server

The time clock server is of course the server that stores and facilitates the company's clock-ins and clock-outs. Make note to how many IP addresses this machine has, as it may share a connection with two networks. Time clock programs can be problematic, and at the first sign of trouble, a certain percentage of people will take advantage of this and try to claim more hours than they have actually worked. Therefore, you want to be particularly careful when it comes making changes to this machine. Having the correct time on this server is important. Computers make lousy clocks. If left alone, not one computer on your network would have the same time. It is standard practice to have this server synchronize with an outside source nightly. I say nightly because I knew of a Network Administrator that set his computer to synchronize with the U.S Navy Atomic Clock at 3 p.m. and by default, at night, the server would synchronize with the Primary Domain Controller at midnight. Because the Primary Domain controller was off by 36 minutes, there were 800 employees paid 28,800 minutes a day, 2400 hours a week that accounted for 124,800 hours a year. If you average that out to about $15.00 an hour, the company lost $1,872,000.00 a year in payroll, not including taxes and overtime. That story is an exaggeration of what could happen. One day, Joe and I changed the time on the time clock in the middle of the day without first thinking about the ramifications. After realizing what we did, both of us thought almost simultaneously, how a couple of well-placed batch commands could produce the above results. With thinking like that, you can see how important it is to keep your computer department happy—I mean your company's time clock accurate.

DHCP Server

A DHCP (Dynamic Host Control Protocol) server dynamically assigns IP Addresses to the computers on a network. This service does not necessarily warrant its own box and this service is typically on a file server or domain controller. You will need to record what address range and scopes are being used. The proper model for applying IP Addresses is by using a DHCP service. It works is like this:

A computer configured to get its IP address automatically will send out a message to the network, requesting an IP address to any DHCP server that can hear it. A DHCP server hears the request and supplies the workstation with an IP address and whatever else is configured in the scope. (Servers typically do not request IP addresses as they are configured with static IP addresses.) The scope might have a Default Gateway, (router) DNS server (Domain Naming Service), and a WINS server (Windows Internet Naming Server). I once configured all of my 43 remote offices on a Frame-Relay network to pass their request for an IP address to my DHCP server at the corporate office so I could keep an eye on what computers were up and running.

E-mail Servers

Some companies have two mail servers; one used for Internet mail and the other for internal uses. Although many e-mail server models will recommend only one mail server, I do not like having the internal mail server exposed to the Internet because a company's most valued information is passed internally. I like to keep this mail server isolated on the inside. Other issues with mail servers are user names. If a hacker can harvest the names on a mail server, than they have half of the combinations needed to crack a network. All that remains is a password. Make note of your mail server's name and IP addresses, as you will need to know this later.

DNS Server

A DNS server (or Domain Naming Service) is one of those servers that do not warrant its own computer but shares with another server, typically. The best and most recommended place for a DNS is on the firewall (providing your firewall is a server). Otherwise, the DNS will reside on your web server. The DNS service provides a list of names to IP addresses for the Internet and your internal network. The www is an alias in a DNS server and is queried by other name servers to resolve your web services. Although it is not immediately important to know your domain information, you will ultimately want to record this information.

Web Servers
I would guess that half of all companies house their own web server. A web server may be either directly exposed to the Internet side of your router or between a firewall. Your web services are within Microsoft's Internet Information Service (IIS) or Apache. Record the web domain names and directories for your reference notepad. Many companies expect the Network Administrator to be the web master as well.

FTP Server
FTP (File Transport Protocol) is generally on the same machine as your web server, and it is used to allow downloads, and uploads from the Internet. Depending on your company's business model, your customers, your sales staff, or just your computer department for accessing software and drivers can use it. Always make note of who has access and who does not have access to your FTP site. FTP servers can sometimes be an intrusion point to your network. Hackers will target this service to install code that executes a remote session; viruses will target the FTP service to store viruses for retrieval after a successful penetration. I once discovered a hole that allowed a file-sharing group to store MP3s for its members. You can see how an FTP site can be a friend and a foe.

What Server Operating Systems Should I Know?

There are several network operating systems out there and each one has its good and bad qualities. Some are better with security, while others are better for speed and connectivity. In my opinion, the best network operating system is one that can get you a job in your area. I know many very stubborn network people that stand beside a NOS (Network Operating System) in an almost religious-like manner. There is nothing wrong with believing in a network operating system that you like, but if no one are hiring Commodore 64 administrators, you might consider learning a more widely used NOS.

The dominant server operating system in your city may not be the same in another. An example of this might be; one area could predominately be Microsoft's NT or Windows 2000 NOS while another might be Microsoft's Windows 2000 and NT4, and yet another town or city might be inundated with a NOS made by Microsoft. It is no secret that Microsoft has the largest share of the NOS market. You may have also already discovered a separation among computer people on which is the better NOS. It is a bitter battle of the operating systems. Unix, the original NOS and the leader for many years, was edged out by Netware, who in turn was edged out by NT, who is now watching Linux take inroads in the corporate market. Then out of nowhere, as I write this, the owners of Unix decided that they have had enough of Linux stealing their customers and filed a suit against IBM for using Linux that uses some Unix code. Occasionally though, there is a break in the battle of the NOS where Unix, Netware, and Linux users gather together and find solace in their unreserved hatred towards Microsoft. If you are reading this, it is because you are looking for an edge in finding a job—you will not find one taking sides in this foolish argument. My advice is to learn what you need to get your foot in the door and have your holy crusade when you have moved out of your parent's basement. Currently, NT Server or Windows 2000 seem to be the most common Network Servers deployed in a company's server room, especially on the Local Area Network (LAN) side. With respect to Novell's Netware and Banyan Vines, if you want to be a Network Administrator, you should pick the operating system with the most market shares, and learn as much as you can. Unix and Linux are typically on the Wide Area Network (WAN) side of the router. These two systems are used as firewalls, mail servers, intrusion detection, and web servers. If you can only learn two server operating systems, which is enough for anyone, make sure you know Windows2000 and Linux.

Rebooting the Server

Rebooting a server is not as easy as just rebooting a workstation. The effects of a 3-minute reboot can be felt across an entire continent. Some companies have entire policies written about when and how a server can be rebooted.

Rebooting a server in the middle of the day can be a monumental undertaking; every department, every user, and every person that looks at their computer sideways, must first be consulted about when the server can be restarted. At such debate, the results go to committee, and only after a signed declaration, will you be able to reboot the server.

Many companies mandate that servers can only be rebooted after normal work hours. It is often desirable to wait until the company closes. Management does not mind that the server is rebooted after work hours, because most computer people are paid a salary and therefore not eligible for overtime.

My approach is a much simpler one. When I have to reboot a server, I use the "Oops" method of reboot.

"Oops, sorry about that. I was updating a security patch and it rebooted itself."

If I have an accidental reboot around lunchtime, it makes for an easier evening for me.

Passwords

Passwords are deployed on computer systems to keep out intruders. Cap locks are deployed on the computer keyboard to keep out computer users. Passwords are also great for keeping out the computer department after calling for help, and then walking away from your computer.

Years ago, I would sit at my desk in the morning and monitor the security log, watching the "wrong username or password" messages scroll down my screen. It was always the same two to three people, every morning, trying to log in with their cap locks on. Because I was the first in the office every morning, the helpdesk phone ringing in the far distance always interrupted my quiet morning. One morning, I had the brilliant idea to just change their passwords in uppercase. The event logs were shorter because of it, the computer users could begin their days feeling less stupid, and my mornings no longer began with me mumbling profanities under my breath.

Most helpdesk or computer support people keep a list of passwords in their heads. (I can remember my passwords and every password that I have ever typed, guessed, stolen, captured, or harvested.) Then there are those people that cannot remember their own single password...ever!

An example of this is Bob. Bob, an office manager and college roommate of our company's owner, could never remember his password, which was of course, bob. Bob called me once a month asking if we could change his password because he had forgotten it again. (Once a month is how often he checked his e-mail) I would do nothing more than tell him that I changed it to bob, so he could remember it. After almost a year of doing this, one day he called and asked if I could change his password to, 925y468x114? I did and he never called again. You just never know the minds of your computer users.

What to Do When a Server Crashes

There is no drug or single event in the world that can make a computer person focus more clearly than when a server crashes. The mere act of a crashing hard drive, database, or server component can temporarily raise one's IQ as much as 50 points. You suddenly become more aware of the universe around you and less aware of trivial aspects in life, such as reality TV, what type of car you should drive, and if wearing socks with sandals is cool. You can for a brief moment, see dimly into the immediate future as your pleasure centers temporarily shutdown and you put your resume on standby for a mass mailing campaign. You move much quicker as time seems to slow down, you can calculate rational and irrational numbers using math that has not yet been invented, and you become a little more spiritual—no, a lot more spiritual. A crashed server sometimes brings a Network Administrator closer to God, his or her fellow workers, and the unemployment line. In a single point of light (pixilated light), when you discover that your backups have not run for over two months, a cold perspiration blankets your feverish body while your knees weaken and the contents of your stomach climb to the top of your reflux valve. This is it; your mission critical server crashed and you do not have a backup. So what do you do next? You do what every Network Administrator does when this happens. You calmly walk into your office, throw up in your trashcan, and slowly begin gathering your personal items while waiting for someone from Human Resources to bring you a box. As you sit at your desk trying to figure out how you are going to get two gigs of MP3s to your home computer, it hits you like a brick—you read this book and configure a redundant backup to another server on another hard drive. Suddenly the feeling in your hands and feet return and you go back to the server room and restore the data.

When a server crashes and you do not have a current backup, you are fired. When a hard drive crashes and you do not have a backup, you are fired. When there is a fire in your server room and all of the company's data is lost to fire, you are fired. Twice in my career, a hard drive has crashed with critical company data on it and I did not have a current backup to restore the data. Backup software is not as reliable as many software companies will lead you to believe. You should pick a day every week to check if your backups are successful. I have made it a habit to check my backups every Monday without fail. Because if you do not... you know the rest...fired.

Another issue with backups is that you do not always know what should be backed up. It is a nice thought to have every drive on every server backed up every night, but in reality, it is just not feasible. At my company, we have every server operating system imaged to a CD-ROM. If the server crashes, we can have another one re-imaged and up before you can restore from tape. Now all that is left to do is restore data files. When you are new to a company, it is almost impossible to guess what should and should not be backed up. The best you can do is back up everything that looks like a data file and bring the head of every department in to show you what they need backed up. The first drive that crashed on me without a backup was the marketing department's Macintosh drive. I did not see it. I did not know it was there and when it was lost, there was someone there trying to monopolize on the situation for my job. So do not leave it up to guesswork. Bring in someone from every department to help you. Later you will be thankful that you shared the responsibility. If your company manager tells you to back up everything, then they are going to have to invest in the proper equipment and storage space.

Types of Backups

Full includes files whether they have been changed or not.

Differential includes all files changed since the last full backup, whether they have been changed since the last backup operation or not.

Incremental includes only those files that have changed since the last backup operation of any kind.

To choose which method of the above types of backups depends on three factors: the size of your tape, the time available for backups, and the length of time you want your restore to take.

A **Full Backup** on a daily basis requires a lot of tape and needs a longer duration to run. I have seen backups that start late at night and finish in the next afternoon, only to pause for a short breath and start again. I do a nightly full backup to hard drive and a weekly full backup and a differential during the other four days in the week to tape. This method saves time and tape.

The Recommended Backup Strategies

Tape Backup:
Most Network Administrators implement a nightly tape back up in four sets. This means that every weeknight, data is backed up to tape in a four-week rotation. This equals twenty backup tapes labeled, Monday1, Tuesday1, Wednesday1, Thursday1, Friday1, Monday2, and Tuesday2 and so on until it ends with Friday4. This way you have a good coverage of the month.

Hard Drive Backups:
In addition to the tape backups, I also like to include a nightly backup to disk, (Hard Drive) stored on a remove or redundant hard disk. I do this for two reasons. 1) It takes what seems like forever to restore from tape (longer if someone is standing nervously over your shoulder), and 2) For the sheer redundancy of it. Once a week you will find that, someone in the accounting department has accidentally deleted a file that needs to be restored or one was corrupted because it grew too big. Backup tapes just take too long for these little files to restore.

Monthly Backups
I also recommend that a monthly backup is performed and archived off-site. We burn a monthly backup to DVD and send one copy home with the owner and another copy with a Network Administrator.

Other Types of Tape Rotations
I have seen the term Grandfather-father-son method, or typically called, Monthly, Weekly and the Son. (GFS) The **Grandfather** backup is a monthly full backup that is stored off-site, while the Father is a weekly full backup that is stored

on-site and the Son is a daily backup that is also kept on-site. This backup scheme requires twenty tapes for a single year.

The **Tower of Hanoi** scheme is a common alternative to GFS that is secure and cost-effective but more complex. This method requires you to perform a full backup on five tapes labeled A, B, C, D, and E. Tape A is used every other backup session, tape B every 4 sessions, tape C every 8 sessions, tape D every 16 sessions, and tape E every 32 sessions, or once a month. This allows for easy file restorations, because you do not have to shuffle through partial backups and it is more cost-effective than GFS because it uses fewer tapes. The Tower of Hanoi method's chief disadvantages are the need for a large enough backup window to accommodate daily full backups and its complexity, which means you should make sure your backup software can automate tape rotation. It is a bit confusing, so do not feel stupid if you do not understand it. I had a difficult time writing it down. I was fortunate in the cases where two of my drives crashed and I did not have current backups, in that on two separate occasions, I took the drives to a company that restores failed drives. I was not fired. It is an expensive business having the data of a crashed hard drive recovered—$5000.00 each. This does not mean that you will have the same luck. Your number one priority as a Network Administrator is to make sure you have current backups stored on and off-site. At my company, we do two nightly backups, one to a tape drive and another to a Snap Server or some other type of external drive. Backup tapes are only good for off-site storage but are slow to backup and slow to recover. Having an additional backup to a hard disk is fast and often more convenient. Because hard drives have become so inexpensive, many Network Administrators only backup to hard drive and burn a monthly off-site storage to DVD.

Troubleshooting

As documentation is a Network Administrator's nemesis, the ability to troubleshoot a problem is his or her best friend. A Network Administrator's number one duty is to fix problems immediately without excuse, hesitation, food, or sleep. In many cases, one will build his or her troubleshooting skills from daily experience. It does not take long with a company before you discover that every server and operating system has its own unique character. When I say character, what I really mean is problems. However, in the beginning, you will not have experience to draw from to help you with your daily, and I mean daily, troubleshooting issues. So what do you do?

Troubleshooting Tips:

- Look in the Event logs for error messages that may pertain to your problem.
- Question everyone that has had contact with the problem server and try to find the last action taken. Nine times out of ten, you can track a problem to one individual. Perhaps it was even something you may have done.
- It is common for someone new to the server room to try to fix things that are not broken, like adding service packs. (Even though every software company recommends installing current service packs, if they are not immediately needed, research the patch. I have installed service packs that shut down the protocol stack on third party software packages.) Until you get your legs behind you, do not fix things that are not broken.

- Ask if any service people (electricians, cleaning service, and other after hour workers) have been working in the building.

- Viruses. Because there are so many types of buffer overflow vulnerabilities always check sites like www.cert.org, www.McAfee.com, or www.symantec.com

- The Internet is the largest resource that you have when trying to correct a problem and you should use it accordingly. Most server and networking problems are discovered by the Network Administrator and then passed on to the software maker for a solution. This is sometimes a slow way to fix your problem and often Network Administrators are left to either solve the problem alone or look to other Network Administrators for help. Most computer people skip the software maker altogether and just go to Google.com and type in either the error message or problem and find a solution in minutes. Google.com is the computer person's first choice when posting software problems and solutions.

Upgrades

Network Administrators are in charge of both hardware and software upgrades. Why would a company want to spend money on upgrades? There are a number of reasons. Companies have to upgrade because they are expanding and outgrowing their current network and software platforms. An example of this might be that your company's accounting department needs a larger platform as their existing accounting software is at its limit. This will most definitely mean a new server, perhaps two, and maybe even a new switch if your company is still using hubs. Every new addition or change to a server room has a direct effect on every other thing. In many cases, you might have to also upgrade to a new server, a new operating system, newer terminals, a new switch, possibly a new router if you have a lot of satellite offices, and what about a database programmer? What happens if the new accounting system is SQL and a SQL programmer is needed for setup and reports? Now you are responsible for hiring a database programmer. There are many instances where the company makes the Network Administrator learn SQL. Scary, huh? Do not worry. You will need to learn many programs that you do not want to through the years.

One of the issues with taking a new Network Administrator position is the existing third party software; they are typically old and out of date, there are not any updates, and its makers are out of business or they will not support it, because they want you to purchase the latest version. Stubbornly, your company refuses and expects you to keep it going just like the person before you. You might even hear, "Well, what's his name didn't have a problem fixing it." You reply, "This is probably the reason old what's his name quit."

Chapter 6

Managing a Department

- ❑ From Tech to Manager
- ❑ Being an IT Manager
- ❑ Pagers / Cell Phones / Laptops
- ❑ Company Politics
- ❑ Purchasing Computer Product
- ❑ Specialist and Generalist
- ❑ The Job 24/7
- ❑ Over-Clockers
- ❑ IT Ethics
- ❑ Confidential Disclosure Agreement
- ❑ Writing Network and Internet Policy
- ❑ Software Licenses
- ❑ Proprietary Software
- ❑ Suggesting New Technology
- ❑ Being Good at Prioritizing
- ❑ The Politics of Getting What You Need
- ❑ The Computer Person Before You
- ❑ Working Without Supervision
- ❑ Training Yourself and Your Staff
- ❑ Working in a Team Environment
- ❑ Communication Skills

From Tech to Manager

It is everyone's career goal to rise to the next level, or at least it is in a capitalistic society. There are countries that do not think in the same terms as we do and are content to remain in the same job until retirement, or between revolutions. I am not criticizing this way of life. In fact, I wish I could be content to remain as I am…but I cannot. To progress is to grow. To propitiate growth you must continually add to your knowledge and training. A football game without goals on each end would be an exercise in fruitless exhaustion. The same might also apply to men and dating. If sex were not an ultimate goal, then a date would be an expressive exercise of patience with a lot of talk about feelings and cat pictures. (I am just kidding.)

From technician to manager is a leap in the natural progression in the field of computers, but not necessarily for all. Manager means less computer work and more paperwork. I began as a computer tech and progressed to a Network Analyst, Network Administrator, and finally to IT Director. Duties dramatically change when you move from technician to a management position and many computer people are not happy with giving up what they love. Here are but a few advantages and disadvantages to becoming a manager:

Advantage:
I like working with computers, so I assign myself projects that I want to do.

Disadvantage:
I have to attend meetings where I translate 1 and 0 into numbers that accountants can understand. Paperwork: managers have to process many reports that other people put into piles and never read.

Advantage:
No matter the condition of a network, a manager can still go to lunch.

Disadvantage:
Hiring staff is a huge responsibility that takes considerable time and resources. Companies often ask you to cut high paying engineers that keep the company running for matters of budget, but later, when this effect is realized, you must produce the same level of people at the same pay rate.

Being an IT Manager

Manager / Executive

There is more to being an IT Manager/IT Director/Network Administrator then configuring nodes. You are a manager of networks, computers, and other IT staffers. Your company will depend on your expertise to help them make purchase decisions and to give advice on future projects. This means that you have to do a lot of research to be as informed as you can when your bosses turn to you for help. Many executives out there honestly believe software is the material used to make pajamas, and it is often your job to educate them without making them feel stupid. Believe me, it is not an easy task to do. Many companies out there will purchase software for their department without your advice or knowledge and expect you to retro fit it immediately without hesitation. I know of a hospital that purchased a $500,000 piece of software that only worked on Microsoft networks. The hospital was one of the largest Netware shops on the East Coast. The software vendor refused to refund their capital. If your company is one of those that purchase software without first consulting you or your department, it is your duty to break them of this. People who make these types of decisions are the same people who will not be held accountable for their actions, and always blame the Network Administrator or IT Director. This has not happened to me, but I have seen it happen to other IT people and it causes a great deal of stress and unpaid overtime.

Pagers / Cell Phones / Laptops

Mr. Gadget must have been an IT person before becoming a cartoon detective, because many IT people carry around quite an assortment of electronics. I personally have a cell phone, 1.5 GIG mini drive, 4 gig mini external firewire hard drive, 512 flash memory, a laptop with two types of wireless connections (because it dual boots into Linux), a digital camera, and 3 blank CD's in the event I have to burn something. An IT person is always on call 24/7. I have my network configured to be accessible from anywhere in the world, with or without my laptop. Just last week I was sitting in a bookstore when I received a call about a database problem in an office 100 miles away. I accessed the bookstore's wireless network, tunneled into my corporate location and from there, the remote office. I rebuilt the database and had the office up again within 15 minutes. Oh, and I have an extra laptop battery and a 60 amp adapter in my SUV. If being ornamented with the latest in electronics and having access to the Internet from your car does not appeal to you...I know, I had you at 1.5 mini drive. As for a pager, I dropped it into the toilet five years ago and never replaced it. (I am not sure that I told anyone about it either.)

Company Politics

Every student that has ever studied networking learned there are seven layers to the OSI Model.

1. **Presentation**
2. **Session**
3. **Transport**
4. **Network**
5. **Data-Link**
6. **Physical**
7. **Applications**

There is also an eighth and ninth layer that have deliberately been kept from you. Why you ask? Because they are company:

8. **Budget**
9. **Politics**

Budget and Politics are the most widely used layers deployed by today's IT department. Finance and Politics are what get you the equipment you need for the server room, the computers for the accounting department, and a hike in your wages. The normal company executives only care about three things: their stock portfolio, company profit margins, and the company's worth. What they do not understand or care about is network infrastructure, outdated servers, or staff computers. From a CEO's viewpoint, these items do not make the company money and are nothing more than a depreciating asset. Assets are how a company measures its worth. Typically, computer equipment depreciates and loses its net worth after five years and no longer reported as an asset or value to a company's bottom line. If anything, computers take away from a company's value because they are expensive to procure and maintain and must be continually upgraded by expensive technicians. If that is not enough, the so called Y2K scare and the expense that led up to the tech stock collapse, made corporate heads even more critical. So unless you can show how buying new equipment is going to save the company money, you had better get used to field stripping a PC, gutting it, and swapping out parts from another machine. These days, CEO's hate everything computer, computer workstations, servers, databases, T1 lines, and especially the acronym VPN (Virtual Private Network). Technology companies that are now either in Chapter 11 or not in business at all overused it.

What About Company Politics

Company Politics (CP) is a hidden monster that lurks within the shadows of every company. Your very survival may depend on your ability to seek out the major players, quickly recognize the hierarchy of power, and adapt to it without anyone ever knowing that you know. CP is when you give an accounting clerk a new computer to replace her old one that died instead of giving it to her boss. CP is when you move a folder to a larger hard drive without first consulting the director of that department. CP has no logical progression or mathematical expression because company politics is a fear-based, primal emotion that uses the same hierarchy order as a chimpanzee troop. CP is also, what a small child says when he or she is tired and ready for bed. (If you did not get that, never mind. You would have to be a parent. "I'm CP...")

Company politics is the most difficult thing to learn for new computer people, because most computer people see things as black or white and do not understand that sometimes things are gray. Every company has its own politics and it is important to try to recognize it as soon as possible when taking a new job. Because so many computer people have such a difficult time, discovering this on their own, it is a worthwhile investment to watch the many documentaries on such cable programs as Animal Planet or The National Geographic channel. Only then will you see similarities within your own workplace and the hierarchy of a chimpanzee troop.

Purchasing Computer Products

Most Network Administrators purchase all of the company's computer equipment and are solely in charge of licenses. However, in very large organizations there may be a purchaser. Whatever the organization, a company's Network Administrator is either involved in selecting product and/ or the purchasing of it. There are accounts that have to be setup, meetings with hardware and software vendors, and negotiating contracts. This is the business end of being a Network Administrator.

Specialist and Generalist

There are two types of computer people: specialist and generalist. A Network Administrator is a generalist. He or she will know 60% to 70% of more than 50 programs, where a specialist will know 90% to 99% of one program in which he or she specializes. This does not mean that a Network Administrator will not have at least one program in which he or she specializes. Because you have to work with so many other programs and networking hardware devices, you sometimes do not have time to keep up with your specialty.

In larger companies, a specialist might be someone who only works on mail servers, security, databases, or even routers. In medium-sized companies and smaller, the Network Administrator handles all of these positions. Most often, a Network Administrator will take a position in a larger company and only specialize in one application. I have a friend who works at Microsoft and only does backups, and other mail servers. My wife used to specialize in Cisco devices. She traveled around the world installing AS5300's and Routers. The company she worked for specialized in Voice-over-IP and selling minutes to the phone company. As with many Telco's (telephone companies), her company went out of business. Currently she is a Network Administrator and has to deal with the everyday hassles of working with people and printers. I am not sure which is worse.

It is impossible to know how to do everything in the computer world, although I know a man named Pete, who is close. Computer users do not understand this and think you should know everything there is to know about every single piece of software on the planet. I put up a section on my website called the "Fix-it-fairy" as a joke, and you would not believe the e-mails I receive.

Generally, as a matter of pride, I know little about desktop applications, such as calendar programs, spreadsheets, or desktop publishing. I am a bonified, certified, practicing networker, and know little in the way of user programs, nor do I care to know. I am afraid that the mere hint of knowing how to turn fonts into a rainbow will kick something out of my head that was difficult to learn. Quite often, a computer user will ask me a question about the program they use; the same program they have used everyday for the past 5 years. Waiting until the last minute to use the restroom, as I often do, because I am too involved in whatever project I am working on, a computer user will stop me in the hallway as I charge to the men's room and ask me how to do something like make their fonts a rainbow color. When I say I do not know, they are almost insulted. I quickly follow it up with, "I am a network engineer and not a desktop engineer," which seems to make the situation worse. In every instance of this, the computer user usually responds by saying,

"What do you mean you don't know? You are IT! It's all the same, isn't it?" They say it every time.

Just last week the CFO asked me how to add the clip art bullets to an excel spreadsheet that was not installed on the computer. I told him I did not know and would send someone down to work with him. He said,

"What do you mean you don't know? What do we pay you for?"

You will get a lot of that as a Network Administrator and you are just going to have to find your own way to handle it without getting angry. I use "Comparative Reasoning" at my company. Because we have many dentists, I often use them as an example so everyone can understand. When I get a statement such as the one above, I will ask, "Why do we have 200 dentists and only a handful do oral surgery and braces? Why do not all of the dentists do oral surgery and braces?

Wouldn't we make more money?" They of course will explain that the specialty dentists have extended training, while the other dentists are generalist. "Well, isn't it all the same?"

When this happens to you, and I assure you that it will, you will have to use your own "Comparative Reasoning."

The Job 24/7

Most computer people are salary-based. This means that you are paid a flat fee that is applied to a 24/7 job. No matter where you are at any given moment, you must drop what you are doing and do the job. The word *salary* was derived from, and replaced the word *slavery,* on September 22, 1862, one day after *The Emancipation Proclamation*

I can not say that I particularly like it, but there are enough "unwritten" benefits that make up for the late nights, weekends, and looking at the CEO's neighbor's computer. Unlike most departments, the IT department does not have someone standing over you with a whip. A duty is assigned to you and you are expected to do it without supervision, and have it completed within a reasonable timeframe. Overtime in many companies means compensation time (comp-time). *Comp-time* means you work overtime hours but not financially compensated for it. You make up the time by either taking the time off, or leaving early. As I said earlier, this is an "unwritten" rule. The IT department might support comp-time, but it does not necessarily mean that it is your company's policy. In some places, it is against labor laws to reimburse your people with comp-time. However, because the entire 'salary' thing has so many gray areas in it, most companies turn a blind eye if an employee has already reached his or her 40-hour workweek.

Over Clockers

When I use the term over clocker, I am not referring to over clocking your computer's CPU. Nor do I speak of cheating on your time clock punch-in. I am speaking of, none other than the geek who will not go home. I call these people *Over-Clockers.*

In the beginning, that is to say, when you get a brand spanking new computer position, it is common to put many hours of overtime to learn the systems. However, many computer people simply do not know when to go home. You have heard the phrase: *Cheaters never prosper.* I have one that says; *Over- clockers never prosper.* The reason for this is because you must have adequate time away from the office or you will go *peculiar.* Many computer people are already on the edge.

There are two types of over-clockers. The first is someone who finds excuses to stay in the office because either he or she does not have a home life, or they feel more in control of their lives at work. It is easy to feel this way. At work, you surround yourself with computers and programs that you control, but over-clocking can also be a trap. I have seen it happen to many people—it has happened to me. You must have a well-defined separation between home and work. Otherwise, you will not want to go to work either.

Another type of over-clocker is someone who puts in evenings and weekends, thinking they are scoring points with their supervisors. What happens in most cases is that your boss does not take notice or does not care, and you become so frustrated that no one rewards you for your hard work that you quit or become disgruntled. Additionally, an over-clocker can intimidate some bosses out there. I have seen or heard of many instances where an over-clocker puts in extremely long hours, nights, and weekends, and then Tom, the laziest man in the department, gets the promotion. Why do you ask? The over-clocker does not know how to get credit for his work. Tom does, because he knows when and where to show up. Over-clockers always come in late because they work late, but this is not the perception of his or her co-workers or bosses. Once an over-clocker does not receive a well-deserved raise or promotion, resentment quickly sets in, and over-clockers turn into an *attitude problem*, and then quit or they are fired. My friend Joe once told me that he believed as long as you show up in the morning with everyone else, make your rounds allowing everyone to see you, you could leave before noon and no one would even notice. He made that statement because he too, was an over-clocker and felt rejected that no one noticed his hard work. There are many people to blame for not noticing a hard worker, but none so much as the over-clocker himself. It is up to them to make sure they get credit for their work, because frankly speaking, everyone else is too busy with their own job to take notice.

IT Ethics

Computer people have the responsibility and confidentiality of guarding their company's data. This means they have access to documents, spreadsheets, databases, and e-mails which other workers are not privy. Surprisingly, most companies do not have any policy regarding nondisclosure. Furthermore, universities do not teach their students IT or computer ethics. It is as if computer people must use their own personal value systems. (I will tell you, knowing some of my friends that can be dangerous.)

Because members of an IT department have administrative privileges and/ or can physically access sensitive company information, does not mean they have the right to read it, copy it, or transfer it to another storage device for later viewing. With no set rules in place, the temptation to access confidential knowledge can be too difficult for some computer people. A click of the mouse can reveal salaries, company financials, stock information, and e-mails…but ignorance is often a better companion than knowledge. Many years ago, a co-worker showed me a spreadsheet that listed all employees' salaries. Once I saw what some of the other workers made, I became immediately resentful. My boss, who I liked, suddenly became an overpaid middle manager that did little to deserve his salary. I went from a happily content Network Administrator to a very bitter under-appreciated laborer.

Unless otherwise stated as part of your job duties, you do not have a right to read classified and confidential company information. If caught, you cannot only lose your job but you can severely damage your ability to get another job. If you cannot be trusted with company data, you will not be able to work in the industry.

I adopted a policy of confidentiality in the computer department that I manage. I drafted a document, which each person in the computer department signed, to pledge that they could be trusted with confidential information. They agreed they would not break the trust of their jobs by reading any company documents, spreadsheets, database information, or e-mails stored or passed through the equipment that they managed. Furthermore, because it is common to unintentionally stumble upon information while working at other employees' desks (company or personal), they also agreed to treat it as confidential. Any breach of confidentially is grounds for immediate dismissal, and could be grounds for a lawsuit.

Here is a copy of the IT department confidentiality agreement:

Information Technology Department Confidential Disclosure Agreement

This Agreement is entered into this ___ day of _____, 200__ by and between *Employee's name* (hereinafter "Recipient") and *Company name* (hereinafter "Discloser").

WHEREAS Discloser possesses certain ideas and information relating to *Company Name* that is confidential and proprietary to Discloser (hereinafter "Confidential Information"); and

WHEREAS the Recipient is willing to receive disclosure of the Confidential Information pursuant to the terms of this Agreement for the purpose of his or her daily duties;

NOW THEREFORE, in consideration for the mutual undertakings of the Discloser and the Recipient under this Agreement, the parties agree as follows:

1. **Disclosure**. Discloser agrees to disclose, and Receiver agrees to receive the Confidential Information.

2. **Confidentiality**.

2.1 **No Disclosure**. Recipient agrees to use its best efforts to prevent and protect the Confidential Information, or any part thereof, from disclosure to any person other than Recipient's employees having a need for disclosure in connection with Recipient's authorized use of the Confidential Information.

2.2 **Protection of Secrecy**. Recipient agrees to take all steps reasonably necessary to protect the secrecy of the Confidential Information, and to prevent the Confidential Information from falling into the public domain or into the possession of unauthorized persons.

2.3 **Unauthorized Access**. Recipient's Unauthorized use or access to Confidential Information will result in immediate termination.

Protection of Secrecy is defined as revealing information discovered in the course of performance of your duties. This includes information discovered while at another employee's workstation, overheard from a phone conversation or another form of communication. Information can include company or employee information.

Unauthorized Access is defined as opening and reading confidential information from other company departments: (Spreadsheets, word documents, database information, and e-mail.)

3. **Limits on Confidential Information**. Confidential Information shall not be deemed proprietary and the Recipient shall have no obligation with respect to such information where the information:

(a) was known to Recipient prior to receiving any of the Confidential Information from Discloser;

(b) has become publicly known through no wrongful act of Recipient;

(c) was received by Recipient without breach of this Agreement from a third party without restriction as to the use and disclosure of the information;

(d) was independently developed by Recipient without use of the Confidential Information; or

(e) was ordered to be publicly released by the requirement of a government agency.

4. **Ownership of Confidential Information**. Recipient agrees that all Confidential Information shall remain the property of Discloser, and that Discloser may use such Confidential Information for any purpose without obligation to Recipient. Nothing contained herein shall be construed as granting or implying any transfer of rights to Recipient in the Confidential Information, or any patents or other intellectual property protecting or relating to the Confidential Information.

5. **Term and Termination**. The obligations of this Agreement shall be continuing until the Confidential Information disclosed to Recipient is no longer confidential.

IN WITNESS WHEREOF, the parties have executed this agreement effective as of the above date first written.

DISCLOSER (_____)
Signed: _____
Print Name: _____
Title: _____
Date: _____

RECIPIENT (_____)

Signed:_____

Print Name: _____

Title: _____

Date: _____

Writing Network and Internet Policy

Another responsibility of a Network Administrator is to impose the rules of the network. You are the sheriff of a virtual territory and what you say is the law. Controls have to be in place for several reasons:

- **Viruses**:
Almost all viruses come from the Internet, so it is sometimes necessary only to grant Internet privileges to those who need Internet access to perform their jobs.

- **Inappropriate Websites**:
Access to inappropriate websites can and will cause lawsuits. You must stress to your computer users that accessing inappropriate websites will result in disciplinary action and/ or dismissal.

- **Harassing E-mail**:
Sexual harassment or cyber stalking by e-mail is a crime punishable by state and federal laws. Always note to your computer users that monitoring of e-mail is a standard process, even if it is not.

- **No floppy disks**:
Do not allow users to transfer data from home and work. These users usually infect the network with viruses. Many employers also do not allow employees to transfer data back and forth for security reasons.

I put together a Computer Policy Manual at my company that the human resource department includes in their new employee package. Every new person hired must read and sign this policy manual. This helps confirm that your company will not tolerate inappropriate behavior in the work place, and helps to protect against lawsuits.

Software Licenses

It is a Network Administrator's responsibility to make sure that your company is up-to-date on all of their software licenses. Many computer people out there think it is all right to steal software from your company. You are not doing yourself or your company any favors by installing unlicensed software. If caught by a software vendor, your company will hold you responsible to avoid a lawsuit, and that entire wink, wink business behind closed doors will not amount to a hill of beans, or basket of feted dingo kidneys. While at work, regardless of your personal feelings for a software vendor, you should maintain a large degree of professionalism.

Proprietary Software

The problem with proprietary software is that most companies have it, you have to learn it, and you cannot put it on your resume because no one else has ever heard of it. You would get a larger response listing every Star Trek movie that you ever have seen on your resume, than you would the proprietary software that you know. There is a very slim possibility that the company for which you are applying also has the same old crappy programs, but I have never seen it happen. Proprietary software is typically programs or applications written just for the intended company. In many cases, a programmer or two is hired, or contracted out to build an application and then let go once the program is complete. I have also seen where the programmer holds the company hostage every time there is a problem. I added this blurb about proprietary software not to scare you, although if you have made it this far and were not frightened, I would be concerned about you. However, there is more than an 80% chance that there will be these types of proprietary programs at a company. If you run into one, do not panic. You cannot learn everything over night and no one is really expecting you to.

Suggesting New Technology

Many company managers rely on the computer department to suggest new technologies that can help their company be more efficient, as well as preventing software companies from talking them into software and technology they do not need. Vendor end rounding happens when a computer supplier unsuccessfully tries to sell you the latest and "greatest" software package and then will go directly to the head of the company. They do this because it works. Fear tactics is the number one sales technique; the Y2K scare did more to upgrade the networks of America than needed. Smart company heads will weigh the advice from the IT department and the company's needs. Software companies are in the business of selling software, not protecting your company.

Know How to Prioritize

When I say, "know how to prioritize," I do not mean proprietary software. (Proprietary software is an entirely different matter that will come later in this section.) Knowing how to prioritize is almost a craft, not like witchcraft, which also falls under a later section titled Cursing Your Computer Users. Prioritizing is necessary when you receive several requests at one time and you must choose which one will be first for the greater good. For example, Gladys, head of the secretarial pool, confronts you and she is frantic over the fact that she cannot print next week's schedule. Currently, you are working on testing your backups and you receive a phone call that the payroll server has crashed. What is your priority? The answer is, of course, the payroll server. This is a hypothetical scenario but you will have similar situations at least once a week. Many computer users have an impossible time understanding that someone else might have a more important problem than they do and will be offended, and will most probably never forgive you for not dropping what you are doing to help them. The mistake every new Network Administrator makes is he or she tries to please everyone at once. Even with the best of intentions, what often happens is you will "over promise and under deliver." Over promising and under delivering is worse than doing nothing at all. You must find an order of priority with what is important to your company and what takes a back door, and then you must let those in your company know what it is. Otherwise, you will just sound as if you made up a reason to ignore them. Below is an e-mail that I sent to my company.

Company Memorandum:

As there are more computers and computer users in this company than the IT personnel can comfortably spit a rat during the rat-spitting contest at the Zellwood Corn Festival (I work for a company in the South), Okay, that is not what I wanted to say. What I really said was this:

As there are more computers and computer users in this company than there are IT personnel, we cannot always help everyone at the same time and must abide by an IT department's order of priority as mandated by this company's owner.

1. The owner or CEO gets first priority as they have the authority to outsource our department.
2. Those who make the company money get the second order of priority.
3. Those who collect the money get the third order of priority.
4. Those who spend the money get the fourth order of priority.
5. Those who make fun of the way our department dresses do not get any help at all.

That e-mail was a great idea because we could refer to it when we were working on something important and someone tried to pull us away for something as stupid as a paper jam in a fax machine. It also stopped that irritating tick sound that a computer user makes with their tongue when you tell them you will get to them when you can. Nevertheless, like in every company, there are those who still think they deserve special dispensation and should go ahead of everyone anyway. It is with these people that we send this e-mail:

If at any time you feel that your needs should go ahead of the IT order of priority list, you will need to present form 2930 completed, filed, stamped and signed by your supervisor, the company CEO, and two witnesses. Please also note that there is a $25 processing fee.

You think that I just make this stuff up.

The Politics of Getting What You Need

Many computer people have a difficult time getting what they want from their boss because they simply do not know how to ask. A Network Administrator might barge into his boss' office, tell him or her that he needs a new $15,000.00 server because the current one is too old and slow, and he is tired of fixing it. His boss immediately denies the Network Administrator's request. He then becomes disgruntled and starts whispering rumors about the company going bankrupt. In many cases, the problem is not with the boss or the company's financial health; it is all in the presentation of the request. The secret to getting what you want is to know how to ask for it.

Perceived Value

Managers, CEOs, and company owners have a different value system compared to a technical minded IT person. For example: spending $20,000.00 for a larger storage device because employees are running out of space to save e-mail might seem important to you, but that $20K shows as an expense, that is really a loss on the books to a CEO. What a logical minded computer person might think is a value to his company, is not necessarily a value to his boss. Therefore, telling your boss that you want to spend $15K on a new server because you are tired of fixing the old one reduces your value and $15,000.00 of the company's bottom line. Additionally, your boss may have to request this expense to his or her boss and you really did not give him or her any thing to validate the expense. When asking your boss to spend money, you should always show a positive value first and the need second. An example of this might be:

"We can save the company $25,000.00 by replacing the old server with a new one."

Then of course, you must show why the cost of a new server will save the company money. Perhaps it is the billing department's server and its down time causes a loss in collections. Maybe it is not a server at all; instead, your company has one T1 line that is always bottle necked and the website is suffering from lost sales. Always show your boss that there is a value in spending money. I like to start with the conclusion first, and then an explanation on how I arrived at it. No one wants to hear a long drawn out explanation before hearing "How much?" Do not turn your proposal into a sales pitch. Your boss can be easily distracted during a sales pitch, wondering where this is going or waiting for you to get to the point. Always make your conclusion first, and then you can precisely state why this is good for him or her and the company.

If however, the server is on its last leg and if not replaced quickly all will be lost, then you only need to show that the value is; you are saving all data from being lost and in order to this you need $15,000.00 dollars.

Do your homework

It is always worth doing your homework before making any proposal. One day, my brother, also an IT person showed me a folder he put together that he was going to present to his boss for a raise. He documented what he accomplished in the past year, how much money he saved his company, and included a chart of comparable salaries for his position in the area. I burst into laughter and asked if he was crazy. He presented his raise proposal, despite my teasing him, got the raise, and immediately sent me an e-mail telling me what a jackass I was for making fun of him. The following week, I presented my proposal. Doing your homework works! Always research your project so you can show how this will affect your company's needs. CEOs want to see how the numbers will affect their bottom line.

Choose the Right Time

Even with the best proposal, timing is everything. Always try to sense your boss' mood before approaching him or her with a proposal. People are more likely to be agreeable and more receptive to your ideas when they are happy and/ or feeling good. Is your boss a morning person, or an evening one? Maybe the best time is when your boss is exhausted and will say yes to anything.

Closing the Sale

When making your request, be positive and confident. Always try to maintain eye contact, and know when to shut up. I have seen people sell an idea to their boss, not know when to stop pitching it, and then talk him or her right back out of it again. When the boss says yes, stop talking because it is a done deal.

The Computer Person before You

Never, I repeat, never bad mouth the computer person before you. It is bad form and you will usually need his or her help with something. Too often, a new hire will take his or her first position and when confronted with something they do not understand, they will immediately blame it on the computer person that they have replaced. You never want to burn that type of bridge.

Most computer people only leave for a few reasons; either he or she was refused a raise or promotion, or because upper management played the blame game with the IT department once too often. Whatever his or her reasons, it will not take you long to find out the real circumstances. There is also a situation where everyone loved the person you replaced and you are going to have to fill a very large pair of shoes. That is okay. In time, you too will be that person.

My last two jobs were replacing disgruntled people. I already knew the rule of not badmouthing those that you replace. At the first job, the Network Administrator transferred all the documented passwords and procedures to an NT 4 server in her office and did not give anyone the username and password. My first task was to break into the server. What I actually did was reinstall a new installation on top of itself and opened the files. On the second job, I got the position while the Network Administrator was on vacation and I was sitting at his desk when he returned. As I walked him to the door, I made it perfectly clear that I had no idea of the circumstances when I accepted the position, and it would not have made that much of a difference because I needed a job. I asked him to keep that in mind in the event that he should come back with firearms.

Therefore, never badmouth the person that you are replacing because you do not know what his or her circumstances were and you may later need that person's help.

Working without Supervision

Most IT people have to come to understand that they are working without direct supervision. This is particularly true with Network Administrators. If you are not a self-starter and do not know how to manage your time or how to plan your week, you are going to have a difficult time. In most medium-sized companies and down, the Network Administrator is the apex IT position. They are in charge of every facet of the company's technology needs, hire the helpdesk and system analyst positions, supervise them, order all products, in charge of the phones, fax machines, and printers and negotiate vendor purchases. I will stop here. In addition, a Network Administrator is paid on salary, so if you do not manage your time correctly, you will be paid the same for 8 hours a day as you would a 14-hour day.

I know many new Network Administrators that will work hard, 70 to 80 hours a week and not get a single ounce of credit for their effort. Not only should you plan your time well but also when you do work extra hours, put in all the unpaid overtime. You had better at least make a big deal about it with your supervisor because no one else will. On another note, most Network Administrators love their work and do not mind working the extra hours. I find myself always having to tell my people to go home.

Working in a Team Environment

An IT department, like any other department, must work together as a team, and all departments must work together as a company. That is a simple plan for a very basic business model. I only mention this because I have seen too many companies where either there is a division in the computer department or the other departments within the company act as separatists. Phone companies are an excellent example of this. There was a time when having to work with more than one department at the phone company was like working with warring tribes. There was no communication between departments and they seemed territorial. I am sure this attributed to many phone companies's financial disarray.

Many computer departments also do not work as a team. I have seen small IT departments divided, each small group unwilling to cooperate with the other, and I have seen IT groups grow so large; they break off into their own departments. Humans are a territorial bunch, and many of us are almost tribal in our loyalties. An IT department that functions in this manner is a dysfunctional department. This is due to the weak management style of its leader.

It only takes one rotten apple to spoil the bunch.

Company morale can be lead by a single person; it can be a happy place to work or a bad one. Sometimes there is always that one person who makes it an unpleasant place to work, and as a manager, you are responsible for a healthy work environment. If you cannot counsel the bad apple to change his or her ways (which you most likely will never be able to do), you must do what all good managers do and give this person a great reference and send them on their way. I like to give a person a chance to find a job because it is easier to get a job when you already have one than to look for one unemployed.

Training Yourself and Your Staff

To keep up with ever-changing technology, computer folk must always keep themselves abreast of the latest hardware and software advances. There are many computer people that are so entrenched with their daily duties on old antiquated systems that when faced with having to find a new job, their resume looks like it was kept in an old wooden chest in their Grandpa's attic. There is a simple rule to follow that helps to avoid a sudden career crash, and that is, always use your current job to train for your next job. In other words, use your current position to help launch your next job, even if you do not want to work anywhere else. These days you have to protect against sudden job loss syndrome.

Keeping your resume up-to-date with current software is good insurance. When you do get a job as a Network Administrator, providing you do not already have one, you still need to consider where you are going from there. I know that I have already given you much to think about, perhaps too much, but even with a job, you have to look forward and beyond your current job. Whenever possible, try to choose products that will be a good compliment to your resume. Select programs that are popular with other companies in a career direction you would like to go. I realize there are ethical issues that can arise from a Network Administrator selecting operating systems and network appliances just to make his or her resume look more desirable, but there are ethical issues with every career, and until there is an actual law, *don't worry about it*. I know four companies right now that did not have ethical problems with outsourcing one third of their IT department to overseas workers.

Training Your Staff

Not only should you keep your networking skills up-to-date, but you should also encourage your staff to keep their skills up-to-date as well. The Network Administrator should also act as a mentor. This makes for a happier, more productive team when everyone is learning something new, studying and taking certifications and testing the latest technology. I have helped make many a Network Administrator. Not like in a laboratory or anything, although I once had thoughts about creating a robot woman in the basement. I still receive e-mail from those who used to work with me, thanking me for helping them advance their career. Even now, I have three of the best computer people that I have ever hired working for me. Not only do I look out for my career, but I try to look out for their careers as well. I am always nagging them to learn this or read that or study for a certain certification. Moreover, they keep me on my toes.

Communication Skills

Because computer people are good with digital communications does not necessarily mean they are good with people communications. I used to say that the difference between an introvert and extrovert computer geek is that an extrovert will look at your shoes when he or she is talking to you. As nice, an idea as it is to think that you will only be working with computers and network gear, the truth is that you will most probably be communicating with more people than computers. You will have to give reports to your seniors, document procedures, and draft corporate-wide e-mails. You will be in no less than three meetings a week and have to give opinions and advice on technology issues. Having good communication skills is as important as good computer and networking skills. If this scares you, I suggest you try improving these types of communication skills. As you will quickly discover from your first job, it would not hurt to take a few classes in how to deal with special or emotionally challenged children. You will see.

Chapter 7

Bitter Facts from Experience

- ❑ Keeping a Messy Office
- ❑ A Word about Computer Part Magazines
- ❑ User's Computer Desk Clutter
- ❑ Cleaning Keyboard and Fans
- ❑ What You Need to Know About Computer End Users *
- ❑ The Differences Between End-users and African Mountai Gorillas *
- ❑ Why do end-users call their computer a hard-drive or modem?
- ❑ End-User Soup *
- ❑ Eating Habits of the Office Worker *
- ❑ Computer Users Mating Habits *
- ❑ Repairing Home Computers
- ❑ Working with Outside Consultants
- ❑ Job Stasis
- ❑ Most Common Mistakes Made By The Computer Department
- ❑ Who has the Power
- ❑ Taking the Emotion out of "IT"
- ❑ Company Birthday Cake Day
- ❑ The Internet is a Living Body *
- ❑ Top 10 Signs that you may be a Geek *

The "*" indicates in excerpt from
TheNetworkAdministrator.com

Keeping a Messy Office

There are two types of computer people: those that keep their offices well organized and clean, and "others." In fact, until two weeks ago upon writing this, I was an "others."

A clean and well-maintained work area tells your employers; I have your data systems safe, secure, and you can count on me to protect them. An employer wants to feel confident that his computer managers are organized and that their mission critical data is safe. This is all due to having a clean office. Unfortunately, with many computer people, this is not the case.

Some computer people keep a messy office. My friend Ian's office has often been described as being a complete and utter disaster area, and by a small few, as being unprofessionally kept. Not to mention pigsty, a disgusting shambles, more cluttered than a garbage pit, and more disturbing than an attorney can comfortably spit a rat that was captured from a pledge pit.

Not that attorneys are known for any special rat spitting abilities; I just like to associate the two subjects because I think this would be a fitting sport for attorneys to compete.

The rest of Ian's office is ornamented with empty computer boxes piled on top of each other, a four-foot high stack of computer supply magazines, and enough computer parts laying around that might suggest a horrific battle among robots was once fought in his room.

Whenever a normal, that is the name given to non-computer people (The actual term for non-computer people is butt-stick. I am just reluctant to use such a vulgar narrative to describe the technically challenged and feel that it is inappropriate for this book—butt-stick—there I said it again.).

Whenever a normal, enters a messy office, the first thing they tend to say is,

"You probably know where everything is."

This is never the case. No one ever knows where things are in a mess. The statement, "You probably know where everything is," is only a polite way of telling someone that their office is a disgusting mess and they are a filthy animal.

Some computer people believe that a messy office is a sign of a busy worker. Only people with messy offices share this misconception. I have seen offices at Microsoft's campus in Redmond WA, with an entire wall covered, to the ceiling, with empty aluminum cans. In times when the industry is short of computer professionals, this was acceptable. When computer jobs are in short demand, employers expect cleanliness and professionalism.

A Word about Computer Part Magazines

Computer part magazines are small sales magazines that advertise the latest computer supplies. These magazines are only sent exclusively to everyone! If you have ever even glanced in the general direction of a computer, five magazines are immediately launched to your mailing address. This techno litter can propagate faster than rabbits. One or two computer part magazines can quickly and easily mound into hundreds, even thousands. It only takes one purchase from an online supplier of computer goods, to get your name on a list that can never be removed. I am still receiving computer part magazines for people that have not worked at my company in 10 years. The "Do-not-call list" does nothing when it comes to computer vendors.

While ordering products from CDW one time, the sales person asked;

"Do you have one of our magazines?"

"Yes, do you need some back?" I answered

"No, I need the number on the back," he giggled.

I am not singling out CDW; it is all of them. This is how they make their money. Computer people love to look through the latest computer supply magazine, myself included. The problem is what to do with them when you are done?

User's Computer Desk Clutter

Many Scientists maintain that time and space warps around stars and black holes. Computer scientists have similar hypothesis that extend before the reaches of time and space involving the density of mass that revolves around a computer user's monitor. This almost quantum singularity is not the product of the minute magnetic field generated by the monitor's cathode tube. This density of matter is created by the end user's personal effects that they use to ornament the computer display like a Christmas tree.

Many computer users attach pictures of their pets, children, to-do-notes, and post cards they have sent to themselves, to their computer monitor. There are snow globes, more pictures of their pets, and coffee cups that say "Worlds Best Mom" stuffed full of pens. There are more pictures of cats, poems of spiritual inspiration, more cat pictures, and poems about cats. Because monitors sometimes go out, it is often necessary to replace them, but they cannot be moved because of the gravitational forces that surround them. This is known as the computer monitor event-horizon.

I have seen companies blame the computer department for not enforcing some sort of restriction on computer equipment. Every computer department should have a computer "user policy" that the employees sign when they are first hired. If possible, try to add a clean computer equipment clause to your company's policy.

Cleaning Keyboard and Fans

Office workers, who eat at their desk, often drop food particles in their keyboards. Hair, paperclips, dandruff and dead skin, as well as other bits of bio matter also litter a keyboard. It is not a pleasant thought, but some company budgets are so strict that you must repair many of the smaller items yourself, and no one wants to have to clean out dandruff from someone's keyboard. These computer users are called *keyboard-polluters.*

Interesting Fact:
This is also known in the computer business as Squirreling. Some end-users or computer users in the Northern regions, unconsciously store food away in their keyboards for the upcoming winter months. The problem is that they more than often forget where they have hidden it. A few bits of crumb here, a few flaky pieces of pastry there, and a lump of soda splat between a key or two.

Desk-eaters, or *keyboard-polluters,* are the more frequent complainers when it comes to computer keyboards, and many companies love staff that sit and eat at their desk because they are more productive. With little support from management, there are matters that you must find a creative solution to; like what my friend Ian does.

Ian is a Network Administrator / Helpdesk Support. (In many companies, there is little designation between the two.) For the chronic *keyboard-polluters,* Ian will make surprise keyboard inspections to embarrass the computer user into eating away from his or her keyboard. Ian will show up uninvited, wearing a pair of surgical gloves, and a roll of newspaper under his arm. He will then politely ask the user to stand away from the desk, and quickly proceed to spreading a single sheet of newspaper flat on his or her desk. Once in place, Ian will take the keyboard, turn it over the newspaper and rapidly shake its contents onto the newspaper. He will then remove a pencil from his pocket, begin examining the debris like a pharisaic examiner, turn, and gives a disgusted look towards the user. Sometimes he will even drop a few items that he has brought with him. After a well-rehearsed display, Ian will carefully wrap up the newspaper, tape, label, and date it with a black marker.

Cleaning Out the Computer Case

Some organizations are dustier than others are. I have seen some dust and debris in a computer fan in a dentist office that could turn even the most resilient of stomachs. In these extreme situations, where there are a lot of air borne particles, computer cases have to be opened and cleaned out.

What You Need to Know About Computer End Users

Once you become an IT professional, never again will you have to fix someone's printer, pull jammed paper from a fax machine, or walk the length of two football fields to reboot someone's computer just to walk back again. The world of a computer professional is a highly technical position where he or she spends most of the daily activity configuring routers, firewalls, servers, and switches. Well, not really daily activities. Truth be told, once everything is up and running, there is not much more you can do then spend a good deal of your time watching network monitors, applying services packs, or taking turns helping computer users. It is helping computer users that I want to address.

Computer users, or end-users as they are more often called, can be the most challenging part of any computer professional's job. End-users can be rude, demanding, and at times, very irrational. They will blame you for their mistakes, not getting enough e-mail or too much e-mail, and are completely without any sense of accountability. End-users will anger you to a boil, insult you to your face, and deject you to your core. It is extremely important that you train your end-users early in the beginning of your job. Otherwise, they will run you to death with their unremitting mistakes. Simply put, training an end-user, means not jumping at their every request. I am not suggesting that you ignore them, only teach them to appreciate your time.

Tips on how to identify different types of End-users

Repeat Offenders – Repeat offenders are those users who are constantly calling for the same problem. When you run into this user, you must resort to memory tools to help them either remember to do it correctly or not call you. If after the third trip to someone's desk, he or she still does not get it, try bringing a work order. Make sure you have the words *violations* or *repeat offender* on it and make them sign it when you are finished. That will be your last trip.

Cleaning Input Devices – Mice and keyboards become dirty when computer users eat at their desk. Almost all computer users eat at their desk. Certain users will always complain about their mice and keyboards not working properly and blame you for continuing to give them faulty equipment. You are not going to get them not to eat at their desk. That is just the way it is. Employers believe that an employee will get more work done if he or she eats at their desk, so you are not going to change this. What you can do however, is teach them to clean their own input devices. There have been times when I have stepped up to someone's desk, laid out a blank piece of paper right in front of them, turned their keyboard upside down, and shook it furiously just to watch all the food particles flurry down on the paper like a snow globe. It secretly cracks me up every time. It is also a good idea to show them how to clean the inside of their mice, making them more responsible for their own equipment. You do not want to waste all of that hard-earned knowledge about computers and networking, cleaning out mice.

Do not know how to use a computer – Many users simply do not know how to use a computer and some companies seem to think it is the computer department's responsibility to train them. I always take a little more time and care with these users. I have a small collection of how-to books for spreadsheets and word processors that I give out. They are less than 100 pages and this puts the responsibility of learning their system back on them.

Knows enough to be dangerous – There are users within every organization that know just enough about a computer to make your life miserable. These users explore the network, change computer settings, and for reasons they are not even sure of, delete system files to free up space on the hard drive. **Solution:** Restrict this user's access to everything.

Time Robbers / Question Stalkers – Time robbers are people who call you for every little incident, and some not so incidental. They call you constantly, e-mail you everyday, and even position themselves outside of restrooms or entrances just to ask you one more question. This user comes in two different flavors; the helpless need to have their hand held and the very lonely that no one else will talk to so they need to invent a problem just to have someone talk to them. **Solution:** the best way to legally deal with this computer user has not yet been discovered. I only mention it as a warning.

My friend Phil says that time robbers are the safest people in the office during an earthquake or tornado because they are always standing in the doorway talking.

I hate computers! – Many end-users are quite proud to make two announcements while you are fixing their problem. The first is, "I'm computer illiterate." To me, this is always an odd confession. It is as if they are trying to qualify their stupidity by claiming ignorance. I do not know what message they think that they are conveying to you, but get used to hearing it. The second is "I hate computers!" Why they feel the need to state this constantly, I do not know. As a side note, computer users call the monitor the computer, the computer the modem and if you tell them to reboot the computer they will turn the monitor off and then on again.

From TheNetworkAdministrator.com...

The Differences between End-users and African Mountain Gorillas

Before I make a comparison between end-users and gorillas, I would first like to apologize to the African mountain gorilla. My first choice was to compare end-users to the inebriated goat herders of the Himalayas, but since I know less about the inebriated goat herders of the Himalayas than I do the mountain gorilla, I have chosen to work with what I know. Although, I am sure that many of my end-users have at times been with a goat, perhaps even sheep. Nevertheless, this article is intended to detail the comparative differences between the African mountain gorilla and the common computer end-user. That may or may not have recreated with Ruminants. My article begins....

1. Gorillas will band together in small family troops and spend their entire lives feeding off the leaves of the forest while protected by a silver backed male that can weigh in the excess of 160 kilograms.

C. End-users will recognize my shoes in the men's room and immediately proceed to ask me questions about their computer. If I were in a gorilla troop, the leader of my group would save me from this humiliation by storming in and inserting enough bananas into the end user's user "end" that he would never be involved with computers again, except while at the proctologist's office, he would have a small interest in the computer that is printing his bill.

2. Gorillas will make a bed of fresh leaves every night before sleeping.

C. End-users will bring in their home computer and place it on my chair without a name or clue to what the problem is. If I were in a gorilla troop, the leader of my group would explain that Doug does not necessarily repair people's home computers because the moment that Doug touches your piece of crap computer, you will think that Doug is obligated to support you and your stupid machine for the rest of Doug's natural life. Then of course, the gorilla leader would proceed in tearing off the arms of the end-user like the limbs of a gum tree.

3. Gorillas are big.

C. End-users have many cats. I do not mean one or two cats. I mean many cats, like a million. End-users have a million cats, each. Therefore, it is easy to see why I say that end-users have a lot of cats. Because that is a lot.... hmm, moving right along.

4. Gorillas have hands as big as my head.

C. End-users have fingers as big as German sausages. This prevents them from ever typing their password correctly the first time. This causes them to ask in that familiar nasally tone; "Is the network down again?"

5. Gorillas are...who cares what gorillas are.

C. End-users make me want to vomit. Not normal vomiting either. The kind of gut retching, dry heaving that can only be caused by something terribly hideous. So much vomiting would occur that, a doctor would have to get involved and replace fluids.

....I may have gone too far with this.

From TheNetworkAdministrator.com...

Why do end-users call their computer a hard-drive or modem?

This is one of the most common mistakes made by an end-user when trying to refer to the computer case. Many times, when they need help with their computer, they will usually refer to their computer case as a Modem, hard drive, or CPU. Usually what they try to communicate to us is something like this:

"Excuse me, I know you are very busy helping someone else, but if you can find the time, could you possibly help me?"

Unfortunately, in most cases what really comes out of their mouths is,

"My modem is not working and it's your fault." Before you are able to translate what they are trying to say, they further their statement by saying: "This never happened before you came to work here." Of course, what they are really saying is, "Please, please mister computer man; beat me in the head with a 9 pound ping hammer so they can replace my five dollar an hour job with an escaped circus monkey with a flagellation problem."

Of course, because you do not speak End-User, you completely misunderstood what they wanted and instead of beating this person in the head with a 9 pound ping hammer, you removed his or her hours from the time clock program, switched his or her social security number with someone that is on the FBI's Most Wanted website and configured his or her mouse for a left-hander.

End-User Soup

In the past, I have been hard on end-users in some of my articles and I am not sure all of them deserve to be bunched in together. This is why, in my infinite wisdom, I have taken it upon myself to create end-user categories. Starting with some of the smarter ones and working our way down to...well, let us just say those that are a little computer challenged.

End-users come in many different shapes, colors, and problem solving abilities. The only thing they all seem to have in common is they complain that their computer is broken, but when you get there, you find nothing is wrong. Below are some end-user categories.

Joke Mailers: Joke mailers are those users who are constantly e-mailing jokes to all of their friends, and searching the Internet for endearing stories that warm the heart. These people typically have pictures of their cats and children around their monitors. Hackers and malicious virus makers depend heavily on these people spreading their cat stories and virus warnings. Late one evening, I once had an opportunity to tag one with my car in the parking lot, but hesitated and lost the opportunity.

Laptop users. Laptop users are those individuals, who always complain that something is wrong with their laptop, but when you suggest leaving it with you to repair; they panic and say, "It's probably nothing." I am reasonably sure that laptops archive the world's supply of porn and these users are sworn to protect it.

Monitor Decorators: This user fancies him or herself as a monitor decorator. They ornament their monitor with so many small bits of debris, there is an actual gravitational shift to the left, and the monitor has to be periodically degaussed. Of course, there are rare occasions that these users are sometimes lost to the presence of a quantum singularity. Abandon any attempt to recycle this monitor for another user. The gooey sticky residue left on the monitor after these items are removed, makes the monitor a better rodent trap than computer monitor. Monitor Decorators and Joke Mailers sometimes interact in same sex partnering.

Paranoid Users: This end-user is extremely paranoid, to the extent that they think you can see them through their monitor. You cannot convince the user that you are not somehow electronically spying on them as they work. You will have more fun, feeding their paranoia by: whenever these people walk past, immediately stop what you are doing and suspiciously follow them with your eyes. Force them to change their password every seven days. Run a defrag program on their system every time they walk away from it. Paranoid users also seem to have a cat or two, although they are too paranoid to display its pictures.

Novice: Novices are those who can perform higher tasks such as changing the desktop, browsing the network for open shares, and knowing how to clear their Internet History. Novices are the most dangerous of the end-users a company can have. They are constantly screwing up their settings, deleting system files to make room for more song files, and are always blaming their latest disaster on Microsoft. Novice users are always reporting the reason their work is not done is because the IS department is always on their computer. It is important to identify the

Novice early so that you can install a more restrictive operating system on their computer until you can get them fired.

Nervous Users: Nervous end-users are those who think that they are going to be blamed for everything. Whatever goes wrong on their computer has the potential of being their fault. They are so afraid of the computer; they must be catered to like helpless children. It is difficult not to be quickly aggravated with this type of user. As a Network Administrator or Help Desk Technician, it is your responsibility--no--it is your duty as a computer professional, to help these individuals seek employment elsewhere. They may sometimes look towards Paranoid User for cat advice. Nervous socializes with Novice who relies on Joke Mailer for advice on personal matters.

Font and Pointer Changers: These users just piss me off.

From TheNetworkAdministrator.com...

Eating Habits of the Office Worker

End-Users are illusive creatures, especially when it comes to watching them eat. Their meals are mainly comprised of a solid block of a frozen protein by-product, which is placed in a microwave and heated until the odor effectively contaminates the building's air exchange. Once this process is complete, the "food" is retrieved quickly and they disappear back into their forest canopy (their cubicles.); only to emerge later to fill the forest with the smell of burnt popcorn. I have never actually witnessed one eating, but I once found a partially eaten box. I quickly rushed it off to my research area to sample their food for myself. Unfortunately, I found it to be tasteless, difficult to digest, and I later suffered from severe stomach cramps. Having no nutritional value, it is still a mystery as to why these people's backsides are three times the size of their cousins that work outside of the office place.

From TheNetworkAdministrator.com...

Computer Users Mating Habits

End-User mating habits begin at the water cooler, continue on to their desk through e-mail, and ultimately end up on an episode of COPS. Having the ability to see into this fascinating world by monitoring their e-mail has given me great insight into a ritual that has never before been documented. Unfortunately, after many failed attempts to document my findings, their meanings are lost in translation without the aid of a firefighter's hose, press on nails, and a bucket of saliva.

Even though I feel I have made great strides in understanding the mating habits of the end-user, I still fear it will be many years before the FCC will be liberal enough for me to demonstrate what I have learned.

Repairing Home Computers

Fixing a user's home computer is the worst sin a Network Administrator can commit. If you let just one person bring their computer to you, not only will you be a slave to that system for the rest of your life, but also word will get out and everyone in the company will bring in their home computer. I have even had people bring me their cable box. Resist the temptation to be nice, because with every favor, there is a certain punishment. I know of some computer people who will charge for just looking at a computer and then charge for parts and labor. Do not do it. There is no amount of money worth what the future holds for you. Your work and home will merge and you will never have peace. Not even, after you leave one company and go to another. If you touch one computer, you are expected to guarantee it for the rest of your natural life. Those of you, who will disregard this warning, will one day look back on this and say, "I should have listened to Doug."

Working with Outside Consultants

From time to time, it is necessary to have an outside computer consultant come to your company and perform work. When this happens, many computer people become defensive and even uncooperative. I have seen it in both company IT person and consultant alike. I have been on both sides in this situation, so I know just how awkward it can be. Computer people are naturally territorial creatures and they will defend their work area to the death, and consultants are predatory animals who want to expose the IT department as being incompetent. At least, this is the contention. What sparks such a conflict is usually attitude. I have seen consultants enter a building, giving off a superiority pheromone, that causes an already on-alert IT department to build defensive walls around the server room. I have also seen the IT department enter into a meeting with the consulting group with a chip on their shoulders large enough to sink a ship. This type of experience can easily be avoided if both consultant and company IT person begin each encounter with an air of polite respect.

Job Stasis

Job stasis occurs when you are stuck in the same job, making the same money, with no sign of advancement in sight. It is easy to find yourself in this kind of comfort zone. Time has made your job easy, you have no stress, and days pass quickly. The problem with job stasis is that if you are not moving upwards, you are not moving at all. I have heard many horror stories where people have given in to the path of least resistance, unchallenged in their job for many years, and suddenly find they are unemployed and so behind on the latest technology that they cannot find another job. No job lasts forever, and in my opinion, you should view your current job as a launching point to your next one.

Another form of "job stasis" occurs when you want to learn more and advance to the next level, but there is nowhere to advance. Some people live in areas where they are fortunate even to have a job. If you work for a company where no one quits or fired, and your only hope of advancement is if someone dies, you might have to move away or consider another career.

Attrition is an example of moving your way up the company ladder without your salary moving with you.

What if you are happy with your current situation? There is nothing wrong with that either. I know a fellow, who came into an IT department at the bottom. The company made many changes that did not sit well with the other IT staff and they all sought jobs elsewhere. With every departure, my friend rose up one more position until he was the department head. In the interim, he studied and passed every certification test he could. With all of the top computer certifications on his resume and a title, he was able to double his salary and then triple it when he found a better job. Some jobs make better launching points to better opportunities than they do actual jobs.

Most Common Mistakes made by the Computer Department

- Repairing co-worker's home computers (See Repairing Home Computers)
- Installing service packs on every computer just because the software company recommends it. Read carefully what a service pack is intended to repair and make sure that this is what you want. If your server is running great and you apply a service pack that fixes a security flaw on the Internet, and your computer does not touch the Internet, reconsider the necessity. I have installed service packs that shutdown network access to third party programs and had to reinstall the server. This applies to upgrades as well. A seasoned Network Administrator will tell you that upgrading software can sometimes be disastrous. If you have no legitimate reason to upgrade, do not do it. Always be suspicious of software vendor's reasons for upgrades and service packs. I once ran across an upgrade that the software maker charged a price and all it did was remove a sub-program as part of a copyright lawsuit. They charged for removing a section ordered by a court.

- Computer makers and software companies are in the business to make money, not to be your friend. Many new computer people are naïve to the fact that computer vendors are out to get your company's money and will say and do anything to make you sign a contract. When negotiating a contract for your company, you must remember that all sales people are liars. I realize it is unfair to say that all of any type of people is the same, but you will be better off in the end if you just assume these people are, for yourself and your company. I have negotiated with corporations on several very large software and hardware contracts, and very few corporations ever did as they said they would. The ones that demand payment in full before their contract is complete are the worst. I speak of very large nationwide software corporations.

Company Memorandum

Just another reminder, it is against company policy to bring your home computer in and have members of the IT department repair it. This company and the IT department will not be held responsible for the loss of or damage to any equipment that is brought in from your home. I have sent out this e-mail on several occasions and there is still some confusion because some of you are still bringing in your home computers. Just in case you do not think that this memorandum applies to you, please read below.

- *You may not bring your computer from home and ask the IT Department to repair it.*
- *You may not bring your computer from home, drop it off in anyone's office, and assume that it will be fixed for you.*
- *You may not ask a company computer specialist about problems you are having with your home computer, and then bring it in the next day to have them look at it.*
- *You may not bring in your home computer because someone in the IT department said hello to you, made eye contact with you, or yelled an obscenity while walking by you in a supermarket.*
- *You may not bring your computer in to work at all.*
- *Under no circumstances are you allowed to bring your home computer to the IT department and have them fix*

it, look at it, give you advice on what to do with it, or drop it off in the IT department and run away.

- *You may not bring in any computer or electrical device and ask the IT department to repair it, make suggestions, or otherwise handle it.*

Warning: *If you bring in your home computer, it will be taken to a local auto demolition yard and crushed beyond recognition and your paycheck will be debited.*

You Must Read This Part.

Just in case you did not read any of the beginning or middle and jumped immediately to the bottom because you thought you read that you could bring in your home computer, you may not. If you do you bring your home computer to work, it will be destroyed at your expense.

Thank you for not bringing your home computer to work.

IT Director / Network Administrator

Who has the Power

If ever there is someone behind the scenes with his or her hand on the button, it is the Network Administrator. In every corporation, when the question is asked, "Who's your daddy?" it is usually answered, "The Network Administrator is your daddy." Network Administrators are often called many names: Network Gods, or Goddesses, computer genius or techno-wizard, the Fix-it-fairy, or the Man. Why do you ask? The Network Administrator controls the flow of information, the storage of data, and the communication with the rest of the world. Network Administrators are the engineers of the company's infrastructure, and when there is a problem, and there is always a problem, the Network Administrator is the first one on the job to fix it. Day or night, on vacation or in the john, we are your lads and lasses. Sometimes, the temptation to peek at data and information that you are not supposed to see is overwhelming and you must resist it completely. While assigning permissions to payroll folders, I once ran across a spreadsheet with the company executives salaries on it. Believe me; such information will only make you resentful. In addition, monitoring e-mail can give a Network Administrator a god-like complex. Some jobs may require you to monitor e-mail for security reasons. I have done so for two companies and even set up monitoring for company owners. You must read e-mail with a steady head and in some cases, a steady stomach. People will say things in e-mail they do not really mean, such as, the boss is cheap. They might do this because they do not want to be the bad guy or gal with someone who requests a raise or something as simple as office supplies. When I setup an owner or executive with the ability to monitor employee's e-mail, I also give them a talk about what people mean to say and not say, and how they should read e-mail. From experience though, I can tell you that almost all company e-mail is the same. The same staff positions send the same type of jokes, cat pictures, and words of inspiration. There are always two or three people sleeping with each other, and at least two are stealing company funds. CEOs and VPs know the best times to go to strip clubs and the poor accounting clerks, who are the hardest workers, have the most personal problems. Occasionally, someone might pop their head up from their keyboard to ask, "Does IT read e-mail?" and you reply, "Yes, yes we do." They laugh, but do not really believe it.

Taking the Emotion out of "IT"

Because many of us (human beings) make many of our daily decisions based on emotions, the world is often a chaotic and confusing place to be, and computer human beings are no different. The fact of the matter is that computer people are more comfortable with computers than they are people, and many do not interact well with others. (This may not apply to you...may not.) From my own experiences, and advice from those much smarter than me, I found that when confronted with a stressful situation, it is often better to wait 24-hours before addressing it. Time will, in many cases, remove emotion from a difficult decision. Many people make the mistake of reacting to a problem with emotional attachments and making the problem an even larger one. The largest killer to a computer job is emotional e-mail. If confronted with an upsetting situation, always try to put some time between the event and response to remove all emotion from it.

Birthday Cake Day

Birthdays are a monumental celebration in many companies. Human resource departments will post dates of birth in the company newsletter. People who usually never speak to you will wish you a happy birthday in the hallway, and then there is cake. Some companies will purchase a cake once a month and celebrate everyone's birthday for the month at once, while others will leave it to the individual departments to handle this most joyous of events. There are cards that need signed and a cake that has enough sugar to damage the pancreas of an adult elephant. It seems that every department in the workplace, except the computer department, practices the birthday ritual. Fascinated by this event, I decided one day to spy on the accounting department as they crowded together and ceremonially cut the cake.

Perhaps I have seen too many TV documentaries, but as I watched the accounting department, I saw a familiar pattern emerge. The first piece of cake went to what was obviously the head of the department, while the others pieces were passed down in a hierarchy of departmental importance. Lowly file clerks received a thin plain slice with no decoration while higher up accountants received larger pieces of cakes with flowers and other decorations. Each person would take their piece of cake and just hold it without taking a bite while stealing small glances at the person that received the first piece of cake. The department head would take a bite, slowly chew it, pause, and then take another. Each time, the rest of the group would wait until she finished chewing before they would eat their piece, always being a bite behind. Watching this, I felt like I was hiding in a duck blind, watching primate's carry out some primitive ritual while on assignment for the National Geographic Society. Then something even more remarkable took place. They used the straws from their diet soda cans and

234

began poking it into their pieces of cake like chimpanzees would a stripped twig into a termites nest...I'm just kidding. However, the whole birthday cake at work thing it a little freaky.

The Internet is a Living Body

In many respects, the Internet is like a living organism. It passes data through its structure using T1 lines, Cable modems, DSL, and analog phone lines just as an organic body transports blood through a series of complex vessels and artery systems. The Internet excretes pheromones in the way of porn sites, and defecates in the way of spam. Popup windows are hiccups and multiple pop-ups can be gastritis or ejaculation, depending upon what website you are on at the time of multiple pop-ups.

Sometimes the Internet catches viruses, but anti-bodies quickly rush in and heal these minor infections. There are viscous invaders that must be isolated and driven away. With each new website, a new neural pathway reaches out, making it smarter and giving it more physical structure. Websites are born and they die, they mutate and multiply.

The Internet reaches out onto the stars using images from the Hubble telescope, and uses web cams like microscopes to investigate itself internally. It is alive with eyes and thinks in digits. For this moment in time, it must co-exist in a symbiotic relationship with humans to help reproduce and expand its reach. Soon, there will come a time that it must expand beyond its confines and venture forth onto the stars and leave us in search of its creators, creator. When that time comes, I hope it takes its bloody spam mail with it.

From TheNetworkAdministrator.com...

Geek Humor

Top 10 Signs that you may be a Geek

1. All of your friends have an @ in the middle of their names.
2. Your best friend is someone who you chat with online but have never met.
3. You see a beautiful sunset and take a picture of it with your digital camera for your computer desktop.
4. When you meet someone from the Internet for the first time in a restaurant, and before you enter, you wish you could save game in case you make an ass of yourself.
5. You finally receive high-speed Internet at home and cancel your phone service.
6. You type "com" after every period when typing.com
7. For emergencies, you have a backup battery supply for your home computer and Internet router, but no food, water, or batteries for your flashlights.
8. You pity people that still have modems.
9. You think it is funny to refer to going to the bathroom as downloading, sex as uploading, and Internet sex as FTPing.

10. You start tilting your head sideways to smile. :^)

Meetings

If you think it is fun, having or taking part in, a company meeting, you are going to love working in an IT department. I have been in meetings that have lasted for hours, only to be late for another. You need to make technical decisions, help explain technology, or provide critical data or an opinion so your bosses can plan budgets far into the future. Expect to attend many meetings. If however, you are as I am, and suffer from issues of a short attention span and are easily prone to daydream, meetings might not be your favorite event. You may have to find methods to help you through these mind sucking, time wasting proceedings. It is important in the beginning to control your eyes from the "glaze over." With time, it will come as second nature to you, much like pretending that you are interested when someone is telling how he repaired his home computer. You will get the hang of it.

Performance Anxiety

When you land your first IT position, you might doubt your abilities and this is a perfectly natural feeling. The fear of not being able to do the job and fired for "Gross Incompetence" looms in the mind of everyone. I can tell you from experience; this is a perfectly healthy emotion and it will drive you to be more dedicated in your profession. Those that do not have this anxiety, are the ones fired for incompetence, because they do not push themselves to excel.

Appendix A

Cabling

Network Cabling

Network cabling is the base for computer connectivity; without cables, computers would have to rely on floppy disks to receive spam and viruses. Even with the great inroads that wireless networks have made, cable is still the standard medium in which networks are connected. It is rather unlikely to have an IT department without cable, and even more implausible to have a career in networking without at least knowing the fundamentals of cabling. In this section, we will look at the different types of cabling used in a standard network topology.

Bulk Cable

Bulk cable is right out of the box cable. CAT5 Ethernet and 100BASE-TX Fast Ethernet is the base networking cable used in most modern networks and any category lower than 5 cannot support the throughput necessary in today's high-speed networks. There are four pairs, (eight wires total) each pair is twisted with a different turn to help eliminate interference from the other pairs, and the tighter the twist, the higher the supported transmission rate. There are seven categories of UTP:

❑ **CAT1**

Category 1, up to 1 Mbps (1MHz) cable. Typically used with analog voice (pots Basic rate interface in ISDN. Also used in doorbell wiring.

❑ **CAT2**

Category 2, 4 Mbps, and typically used in an IBM Cabling system for Token Ring Networks.

❑ **CAT3**
Category 3, 16 Mbps, and typically used with voice and data on 10BASET Ethernet.

❑ **CAT4**
Category 4, 20 Mbps, and typically used in a Token Ring network

❑ **CAT5**
Cat5 refers to category 5 data cabling, which is a 4 pair cable (8 wires) 100 Mbps cable. Typically used in an Ethernet network.

❑ **CAT5e**
Category 5e 1000 Mbps, used with ATM Gigabit Ethernet.

❑ **CAT6**
Category 6 cabling, used in fast broadband networks up to 400 MHz

❑ **CAT6e**

Category 6e supports 10 Gigabit Ethernet

❑ **CAT7**

Category 7, 600-700 MHz. This cable can be used with full-motion video.

Unshielded Twisted Pair (UTP)

Twisted pair cabling comes in two types: shielded and unshielded. Unshielded twisted pair (UTP) is the most popular because of it price point and is used on most data networks. Twisted Pair is a network standard and are 10 Mhz 10BASE-T to 100BASE-T. With the raise of high-speed networking, many IT professionals are laying CAT5e, 1000BASE-T cable, for future needs with ATM Gigabit networks.

Shielded Twisted Pair (STP)

Shielded Twisted Pair protects against EMI interference than does unshielded wires. STP is stiffer and more difficult to run because of the material used for the shielding. STP is a better cable to use, however the cost often does not justify the additional experience and is passed over for unshielded cable.

Screened Twisted Pair

Screened Twisted Pair (ScTP) is 4-pair 100 ohm UTP, with a single foil or braided screen surrounding all four pairs in order to minimize EMI radiation and susceptibility to outside noise. Screened twisted pair is also called Foil Twisted Pair (FTP), or Screened UTP.

Standard Ethernet Patch Cable

A data patch cord, or cable, is used with an Ethernet connection as "straight-through." This means that pin 1 of the connector end of the plug on one end is connected to pin 1 on the plug of the other end; the wires are straight through. Only wires 1, 2, 3, and 6 are used to transmit a signal, while the other 4 wires go unused. If you hold the two-connector ends of a patch cord together, side-by-side, with the clip down, from left to right the color of the wires should be the same across. In our next example, you can see the active wires and colors.

<u>Straight-through</u>

```
Pin       color          pair   name
---       -----          ----   --------
1         white/orange   2      TxData +
2         orange         2      TxData -
3         white/green    3      RecvData +
4         blue           1
5         white/blue     1
6         green          3      RecvData -
7         white/brown    4
8         brown          4
```

RJ-45 Connector (Registered Jack)

The standard connector for twisted pair cabling is an RJ-45 connector. An RJ-45 looks like a large phone connector. (A phone connector is a RJ-11) RJ stands for Registered Jack.

Crossover Cables

The simplest of LAN wiring is two computers directly connected to each other using a crossover cable. A crossover cable is just that; instead of the 4 pairs (8 wires) of wires inside a standard 100BASE-T cable being straight through from one end to the other, the wires are crossed over like in the next example.

Crossover cable configuration:

Standard End	Crossover End
Pin 1 White/Orange	Pin 1 White/Green
Pin 2 Orange	Pin 2 Green
Pin 3 White/Green	Pin 3 White/Orange
Pin 4 Blue	Pin 4 Blue
Pin 5 White/Blue	Pin 5 White/Blue
Pin 6 Green	Pin 6 Orange
Pin 7 White/Brown	Pin 7 White/Brown
Pin 8 Brown	Pin 8 Brown

Crossover cables are used to connect two computers together without the use of a hub, or need to connect to hubs, or switched together. It should be stressed though, that most modern hubs and switches are self-sensing and may not require a crossover cable.

Coaxial Cable

Coaxial cable has a single copper core at the center, surrounded with a plastic layer of insulation wrapped with a braided metal shielding. The metal shield helps reduce the EMI radiation from fluorescent light and other forms of electro magnetic interference. The metal shield helps reduce the EMI from fluorescent light and other forms of electro magnetic interference.

Thicknet

Thicknet coax is a dated medium, 1 cm thick (50-ohm) and is known as 10base5. 10base5 Ethernet supports 10 Mb/s transmission rate over a maximum 500-meter length. The outer jacket of Thick Ethernet cables is typically a bright color (often yellow) with black bands at 2.5-meter intervals to mark valid transceiver placement points. 10Base5 transceivers are attached through a clamp that makes physical contact with the cable. These transceivers are also called "transceiver taps" because they are connected through a process known as "tapping" that bits a hole in the cable to allow contact. This method of tap is a non-intrusive connection because the tap can be made on an active network without disrupting traffic flow. For more information on Thicknet cabling, go to your local used bookstore, or other forms of antiquated knowledge that you will never use.

Thinnet

Thinnet is also 50-ohms, but half that of Thicknet. (5mm) Thinnet looks like the same medium used as the cable on your cable box, but has a lower ohms rating. Thinnet is used with Ethernet 10Base2, and supports 10 Mb/s transmission rate over 185-meter maximum. Thinnet uses BNC connector that connects to a T-connector. If a T-connector is the last computer on the network then a 50-ohm end terminator must be attached.

Fiber Optic

Fiber optic cabling is the backbone of the Internet. Fiber optic cabling is buried beneath every major city, crosses every continent, and spans across the ocean's floors. Fiber optics signaling is modern technology's Morse code for high-speed communications. Fiber cabling has a low loss, high bandwidth than can be used over greater distances than copper cables. In data networks, this can be as much as 2km without the use of repeaters.

Fiber optic cabling transmits optical signals through a thin glass fiber. How it works is; an electrical signal is converted at the head of the fiber cable to optical signals, (or light flashes that represent ones and zeros) that pass through the cable and is re-converted at the other end back into electrical signals. Three concentric layers construct fiber optic cabling. The "core" is the center of the cable in which light is transmitted through. The "cladding" is what confines the light to the core, and the outer buffer, or "protective layer" protects the center cable. Typically Kevlar®, the same material used in bulletproof jackets, is used to protect the fiber optic core.

Light travels along a fiber cable by a process called 'Total Internal Reflection' (TIR); this is made possible by using two types of glass, which have different refractive indexes. The inner core has a high refractive index and the outer cladding has a low index.

There are two types of Fiber Optic Cabling: Single Mode Fiber Optic Cable, and Multimode.

Single Mode fiber optic cable is primarily used as an interbuilding backbone cable. It is well suited for distances up to 3 km, and delivers data at a rate up to 10 Gbps. Single mode fiber optic cable is used for long distance applications that require high bandwidth.

Multimode fiber optic cable

FOIRL, 10Base-FL, 10Base-FB, 10Base-FP, 100Base-FX, 1000Base-LX, and 1000Base-SX are the Ethernet media used with fiber optic cabling.

Appendix B

Computer and Networking Terms and Definitions

A

Access Control – Access Control ensures that resources connections are only granted to those users who have privilege to them.

Access Control List (ACL) – An access control list (ACL) is a table that tells a computer operating system which access rights each user has to a particular system object, such as a file directory or individual file.

Account Harvesting
Account Harvesting is the process of gathering account names on a system. Spammers typically harvest e-mail addresses from websites and phishing.

Active Content
Embedded code (Java, ActiveX) inside a web page that is downloaded and executed.

Activity Monitors
Activity monitoring is a process that scans and prevents virus infection. The process uses known viruses and algorithms to protect a company network infrastructure.

Address Resolution Protocol (ARP)
Address Resolution Protocol (ARP) is a protocol for mapping an Internet Protocol address to a physical machine address. A local router or routing table caches the ARP number of any given node that it can see on the network.

Algorithm

A finite set of well-defined instructions for a problem solving or accomplishing a computation procedure.

Alpha

A RISC architecture developed by Digital Equipment Corporation.

Applet

Applets are typically referred to in Java programs. A client's browser may execute an applet that might execute a larger program on the server.

ARPANET

Advanced Research Projects Agency Network, of the U.S. Department of Defense, pioneered packet-switched network, designed and build in the early 1970s. In June 1990, the ARPANET became today's Internet.

ASCII

American Standard Code for Information Interchange; is the standard character-coding scheme used by most computers to display letters, digits and special characters.. There are 128 standard ASCII codes each of which can be represented by a 7 digit binary number: 0000000 through 1111111.

ATAPI

ATAPI is the protocol used by CD-ROM drives use to communicate with the computer.

Auditing

Auditing is the gathering of information to ensure guidelines are meet in either security or software licensees.

Authentication

The process of identifying an individual, usually based on a username and password. In security systems, authentication is distinct from authorization , which is the process of giving individuals access to system objects based on their identity. Authentication merely ensures that the individual is who he or she claims to be, but says nothing about the access rights of the individual.

Authoring Tools
HTML editors, document conversion tools, tools that generate Web content from databases are all authoring tools

Authorization
Authorization must be met before approval, or permission is granted to access programs, files or folders on a computer system.

B

Backbone
A central high-speed network that connects smaller, independent networks to larger networks.

Backdoor
A backdoor is a hidden access path to a computer system. Trojans can open up a backdoor, as can a rootkit.

Backwards Compatible
A design that continues to work with earlier versions of a language, program, etc.

Bandwidth
Bandwidth is a term used to describe the capacity of a communication channel to pass data through in a given amount of time. Expressed in bits per second.

Basic Authentication
Basic Authentication is the simplest web-based authentication used to pass username and passwords.

Baud

The number of changes in signal per second. A signal with four voltage levels may be used to transfer two bits of information for every baud.

BBS (Bulletin Board System)

Popular in the 1990's, BBS boards were used as discussion boards, and to upload and download files, much like today's chat rooms. Run on digiboards and phone lines, BBS's became too slow. Law enforcement shutdown many BBS's because of pirating.

Binary

The "0" and "1" numbering system that computers use to communicate from program to hardware.

BIND

BIND is an acronym for Berkeley Internet Name Domain, an implementation of DNS. DNS is for domain name to IP address resolution.

BIOS

(BIOS) Basic Input-Output System is a chip (or set of chips) in a computer that controls how your computer communicates with some of the basic hardware components in your system, such as the keyboard, floppy drive, and hard disk.

Bit

The smallest unit of information storage; a contraction of the term "binary digit;" one of two symbols—"0" (zero) and "1" (one) - that are used to represent binary numbers.

Boot

Boot is the process or starting your computer

Boot Record

The boot record on a hard drive, or floppy disk, is at the beginning of the disk. The boot record is on the active or bootable partition and contains the start up information that boots the operating system.

Boot Record Infector

A boot record infector is a piece of malware that inserts malicious code into the boot sector of a disk.

Border Gateway Protocol (BGP)

The Border Gateway Protocol is an exterior gateway protocol defined in RFC 1267 and RFC 1268. It's design is based on experience gained with EGP, as defined in STD 18, RFC 904, and EGP usage in the NSFNET Backbone, as described in RFC 1092 and RFC 1093. See also: Exterior Gateway Protocol

Bridge

A device that supports LAN-to-LAN communications. Bridges may be equipped to provide frame relay support to the LAN devices they serve. A frame-relay-capable bridge encapsulates LAN frames in frame relay frames and feeds those frame relay frames to a frame relay switch for transmission across the network.

British Standard 7799

A standard code of practice that provides guidance on how to secure information systems. British Standard 7799 includes a management framework, objectives, and control requirements for information security management systems.

Broadcast

To simultaneously send the same message to all nodes on a local segment.

Broadcast Address

An address used to broadcast a datagram to all hosts on a given network using UDP or ICMP protocol.

Browser

A client computer program that translates and displays HTML code.

Brute Force

A hacking method used to find passwords or encryption keys by trying every possible combination of characters until the code is broken.

Buffer Overflow

This happens when more data is put into a buffer or holding area, then the buffer can handle. This is due to a mismatch in processing rates between the producing and consuming processes. This can result in system crashes or the creation of a back door leading to system access.

Byte

A set of Bits that represent a single character. Usually there are 8 Bits in a Byte.

C

Cache

Similar to a buffer. All or part of a file may be read to a cache in RAM, then used from RAM rather than requiring access from disk. An optional file on your hard drive where such data also can be stored

Cache Poisoning

Malicious or misleading data from a remote name server is saved [cached] by another name server. Typically used with DNS cache poisoning attacks.

Caplocks

Caplocks are a key on a standard keyboard that prevents one third of the worlds computer users from logging onto their computers each morning.

CAT1

Category 1, up to 1 Mbps (1MHz) cable. Typically used with analog voice (pots) Basic rate interface in ISDN. Also used in door bell wiring.

CAT2

Category 2, 4 Mbps, and typically udes in an IBM Cabling system for Token Ring Networks.

CAT3

Category 3, 16 Mbps, and typically used with voice and data on 10BASET Ethernet.

CAT4

Category 4, 20 Mbps, and typically used in a Token Ring network

CAT5

Cat5 refers to category 5 data cabling, which is a 4 pair cable (8 wires) 100 Mbps cable. Typically used in an Ethernet network.

CAT5e

Category 5e 1000 Mbps, used with ATM Gigabit Ethernet.

CAT6

Category 6 cabling, used in fast broadband networks up to 400 MHz

CAT6e

Category 6e supports 10 Gigabit Ethernet

CAT7

Category 7, 600-700 MHz. This cable can be used with full-motion video.

Cell

A cell is a unit of data transmitted over an ATM network.

Certificate-Based Authentication

Certificate-Based Authentication is used to authenticate and encrypt HTTP traffic, using SSL certificates.

CGI

Common Gateway Interface, an interface that connects the Web with other software and databases. CGI defines how data is passed from a server to a CGI program and has nothing to do with the programming language itself. Hence CGI programs can be written in a variety of languages (such as C, Pascal, Perl, etc).

Chain of Custody

Chain of Custody is the federal rules that govern the handling of evidence.

Challenge-Handshake Authentication Protocol (CHAP)

An authentication method that can be used when connecting to an Internet Service Provider. CHAP allows you to login to your provider automatically, without the need for a terminal screen.

ChRoot

"chroot-ed" is the usual term in the Unix world to say that users are kept in a confined part of the directory tree. Trying to change to a directory outside of this limited area will fail.

Checksum

A value that is computed and that depends on the contents of a set of data. Checksum is used to detect if the data has been altered during transmission or when being stored and properly retrieved.

Cipher

A cryptographic algorithm for encryption and decryption.

Ciphertext

The result after Plaintext is passed through a Cipher.

Circuit Switched Network

A circuit switched network is where a single continuous physical circuit connected two endpoints.

Clock Speed

Clock speed is the rate at which a computer processor can complete a processing cycle.

Clone

The term clone as referred to in computers arose in the mid-80s to describe a Windows based PC, not manufactured by IBM. Dells, HP, Compaq, were all considered as clones. These days, clones are no name computers assembled by hand.

Collision

A collision occurs when multiple systems transmit simultaneously on the same wire.

CMOS

Originally CMOS was abbreviation for Complementary Metal Oxide Semiconductor; a semiconductor technology used in integrated circuits. CMOS is now described as the low-level hardware BIOS setting, and the computer's clock

Competitive Intelligence

Competitive Intelligence is espionage using legal mean.

Computer Emergency Response Team (CERT)

The CERT was formed by DARPA in November 1988 in response to the Internet worm incident. CERT responds to computer security events that occur on Internet. 24-hour telephone Hotline for reporting Internet security issues is (412) 268-7090. www.cert.org

Cookie

A cookie is a piece of data that is exchanged between a web server and a users browser. A cookie may be a text file placed on the client's computer with information stored from the last visit.

Cron

Cron is a Unix and Linux application that runs scheduled jobs.

Crossover Cable

A crossover cable reverses the pairs of cables at the other end and can be used to connect devices directly together.

Connector 1 Pin Out	Connector 2 Pin Out
1 2 3 4 5 6 7 8	3 6 1 Open Open 2 Open Open

Crosstalk

Crosstalk is the coupling of unwanted signals from one pair within the same cable to another pair.

Cryptanalysis

The mathematical science that deals with analysis of a cryptographic system in order to gain knowledge needed to break or circumvent the protection that the system is designed to provide. In other words, convert the cipher text to plaintext without knowing the key.

Cryptographic Algorithm or Hash

An algorithm that employs the science of cryptography, including encryption algorithms, cryptographic hash algorithms, digital signature algorithms, and key agreement algorithms.

Cryptography

Cryptography encrypts data so anyone that intercepts it can not openly read the message files.

Cut-Through

Cut-Through is a method used in data switching where only the header of a packet is read before it is forwarded to its destination. Routers and Switches will use Cut-through.

Cyclic Redundancy Check (CRC)

Sometimes called "cyclic redundancy code". CRC is a mathematically generated number that data receivers use to verify the proper bit arrangement in a bit stream
Daemon

D

Daemon

A program that runs in the background without supervision. This is typically associated with Unix and Linux systems.

Database Compression

Storing data in a format that requires less space than usual. Compressing data is the same as packing data. Data compression is particularly useful in communications because it enables devices to transmit the same amount of data in fewer bits (requiring less time). There are a variety of data compression techniques, but only a few have been standardized.

DBMS
Database Management System

Data Encryption Standard (DES)
A widely-used method of data encryption using a private key.

Data Aggregation
The process of redefining data into a summarization based on some rules or criteria.

Data Mining
The ability to query very large databases in order to satisfy a hypothesis.

Data Owner
A Data Owner is the entity having responsibility and authority for the data.

Data Warehousing
A data warehouse brings together data from multiple transactional systems and enables users to access and analyze the information at various levels.

Datagram
A data packet used by a connectionless, unsequenced protocol like IP and UDP. A datagram may be encapsulated in one or more packets passed to the data link layer.

Decibel (dB) A logarithmic measure of the ratio of two signal levels:

Decoupling-network An electrical circuit that prevents test signals that are applied to the unit under test from affecting other devices, equipment, or systems that are not under test

Decapsulation
Decapsulation is the process of stripping off one layer's headers and passing the rest of the packet up to the next higher layer on the protocol stack.

Decryption
Decryption is the process of transforming an encrypted message into its original plaintext.

Denial of Service
(DoS) When a hacker performs a Denial Of Service attack against web servers, FTP servers, and mail servers. Pinging a server with large ping packets is a form of DoS.

DHTML
Dynamic HTML, a mixture of standards including HTML, style sheets, the Document Object Model and scripting. However, there is no World Wide Web Consortium specification that formally defines DHTML.

Dictionary Attack
An attack that uses a word dictionary to crack a password or key. A dictionary is typically a text file that contains common words and phrases used as passwords.

Digital Envelope
A digital envelope is an encrypted message with the encrypted session key.

Digital Signature Algorithm (DSA)
An asymmetric cryptographic algorithm that produces a digital signature in the form of a pair of large numbers.

Digital Signature Standard (DSS)
A US Government standard that specifies the Digital Signature Algorithm (DSA), this involves asymmetric cryptography.

Disassembly
The process of taking a binary program and extrapolating the source code from it.

Disaster Recovery Plan (DRP)
A plan by the IT department to recovery lost data in the event of a systems crash or disaster.

Disk Druid
Disk Druid is a component of the Red Hat Linux installation, which is used to partition drives.

Distance Vector
Distance vector is the measurement or the cost of routes; this determines the best-known route to send a data packet by the router.

Domain
On the Internet, a domain consists of a set of network addresses. In the Internet's domain name system, a domain is a name with which name server records are associated that describe sub-domains or host. In Windows NT and Windows 2000, a domain is a set of network resources (applications, printers, and so forth) for a group of users.

Domain Name
A name that identifies one or more IP addresses. For example, the domain name microsoft.com represents about a dozen IP addresses. Domain names are used in URLs to identify particular Web pages. For example, in the URL http://www.microsoft.com/index.html, may be the domain name Microsoft.com

Domain Name Service (DNS)
DNS is a naming service that translates IP Addresses into friendly name (www.whatever.com) to identify servers on a network.

Download
To copy data from a main source to a local device. The term is often used to describe the process of copying a file from an Internet server to one's own computer. Downloading can also refer to copying a file from a network file server to a computer on the network.

DSL
Digital Subscriber Link technologies, use sophisticated modulation schemes to pack data onto copper wires. They are sometimes referred to as last-mile technologies because they are used only for connections from a telephone switching station to a home or office, not between switching stations.

Dual Boot
A computer configuration with a choice of two operating systems to boot from.

Due Diligence
Due diligence is the required procedure that organizations must develop and deploy as a protection plan to prevent fraud, abuse, and additional deploy a means to detect them if they occur.

DumpSec
DumpSec is a security tool that dumps a information about a system's users, file system, registry, permissions, password policy, and services.

Dumpster Diving
Dumpster Diving is a practice of rummaging through trash to obtain passwords from corporate and private dumpsters.

Dynamic Link Library
A file containing executable code and data bound to a program at load time or run time, rather than during linking. Several applications can share the code and data in a dynamic link library simultaneously. (usually referred to as a DLL file).

Dynamic Routing Protocol
Dynamic Routing Protocols learn routes. (RIP, EIGRP) Routers to update their routing tables perform dynamic routing. Dynamic Routing Protocol occurs when routers talk to adjacent routers, informing each other of what networks each router is currently connected to.

E

Eavesdropping
Eavesdropping is simply listening to a private conversation, which may reveal information that can provide access to a facility or network.

Echo Reply
An echo reply is the response a machine that has received an echo request sends over ICMP. Ping is a typical Echo reply response.

Echo Request
The Echo Reply is an ICMP message generated in response to an ICMP Echo Request message, and is mandatory for all hosts and routers. Ping is a typical Echo Request response.

Egress Filtering
Filtering outbound traffic.

EIDE
Enhanced Integrated Drive Electronics is a newer version of the IDE Interface standard.

Encapsulation
The technique used by layered protocols in which a layer adds header information to the protocol data unit (PDU) from the layer above.

Encryption
Cryptographic transformation of data (called "plaintext") into a form (called "cipher text") that conceals the data's original meaning to prevent it from being known or used.

Ephemeral Port
In computing, a port (derived from seaport) is usually an interface through which data are sent and received. An exception is a software port (derived from transport), which is software that has been "transported" to another computer system (see below for details).

Escrow Passwords
Escrow Passwords are passwords written down and stored in a secure location (like a safe). This allows emergency personnel to access log-ons when privileged personnel are unavailable.

Ethernet
The most widely installed local area network technology used. Ethernet is a specified standard, (IEEE 802.3) An Ethernet LAN typically uses Category 5 cable, although in past installations, coax and CAT3 was the standard. Devices are connected to the cable and compete for access using the CSMA/CD protocol.

Exposure
Sensitive data directly released to an unauthorized entity. This could be a security vulnerability from software configurations, or from an inside source such as a disgruntled employee.

Extended ACLs (Cisco)
Extended ACLs are an extended form from the Cisco Standard ACLs on Cisco routers. They can make filtering decisions based on IP addresses (source or destination), Ports (source or destination), protocols, and whether a session is established.

Exterior Gateway Protocol (EGP)
EGP is a protocol used to distribute routing information to routers from autonomous systems.

F

FAQ
Frequently Asked Questions, usually associated with Usenet newsgroups but often featured on Web sites also, the FAQ is a list of questions commonly asked by users.

False Rejects
False Rejects are when an authentication computer or system fails to recognize a valid user.

Fdisk
Fdisk is a partition utility that creates, modifies, and deletes partitions.

File Transfer Protocol (FTP)
FTP is an Internet protocol that is used to transfer files. Anonymous FTP allows you to connect remotely to computers to transfer and receive files publicly.

Filesystem
Filesystems are unique to operating systems and cannot be read between them. Linux supports multiple filesystems.

Filter

A filter typically refers to a firewall or sniffer method of analyzing and distributing packets.

Filtering Router

A filtering router may be used as a firewall or part of a firewall. A router usually receives a packet from a network and decides where to forward it on a second network

Finger

Finger is an Internet protocol that allows you to check a user's login information. Finger, originally a Unix protocol, takes an e-mail address and returns information about the user who owns that e-mail address.

Fingerprinting

Sending queries to a system in order to determine the operating system. Fingerprinting can also be characterized as a method of determining a systems naming and operating systems convention.

Firewall

A computer hardware device or software, used to prevent the unauthorized access to a network.

Flooding

A process of becoming overwhelmed my intrusive and erroneous data to interrupt or take control of a system.

Formatting

Forest

A forest is a set of Active Directory domains that replicate their databases with each other.

Fork Bomb

A Fork Bomb, also known as a "logic bomb" works by using the fork() call to create a new process which is a copy of the original. This is typically an attack on Unix systems. By doing this repeatedly, all available processes on the machine can be taken up. It is similar to having a computer make copies of the same files in a new directory until there is no more space on the hard drive.

Forward Lookup
Forward lookup uses an Internet domain name to find an IP address by using DNS.

Fragment Overlap Attack
A TCP/IP Fragmentation Attack is possible because IP allows packets to be broken down into fragments for more efficient transport across various media. The TCP packet (and its header) and is carried in the IP packet. In this attack the second fragment contains incorrect offset. When packet is reconstructed, the port number will be overwritten.

Fragmentation
Scattering of data over a hard disk caused by successive recording and deletion operations. Generally this will eventually result in slow data recall.

Frames
Data that is transmitted between network points as a unit complete with addressing and necessary protocol control information. A frame is usually transmitted serial bit by bit and contains a header field and a trailer field that "frame" the data. A frame is also a term used in html code used to display content inside the same browser without opening a new browser or changing the existing page.

Full Duplex
The ability of a device or line to transmit data simultaneously in both directions. Phones with half duplexing sound choppy when both parties try to talk at once.

Fully-Qualified Domain Name
A fully-qualified domain name (FQDN) includes all parts of a domain, the hostname or subdomain, the domain, and the top-level domain. They are often seen in the URLs for websites.

G

Gateway
A hardware or software set-up that translates between two dissimilar protocols, or networks.

gethostbyaddr
The gethostbyaddr DNS query is when the address of a machine is known and the name is needed.

gethostbyname
The gethostbyname DNS quest is when the name of a machine is known and the address is needed.

GID
Short for Group ID

Gopher
A system that pre-dates the World Wide Web for organizing and displaying files on Internet servers. A Gopher server presents its contents as a hierarchically structured list of files.

GNU
GNU is a Unix-like operating system that comes with source code that can be copied, modified, and redistributed. The GNU project was started in 1983 by Richard Stallman and others, who formed the Free Software Foundation.

Gnutella
An Internet file sharing utility. for peer-to-peer sharing of data between computers (typically MP3 music files).

H

Hacker
Hacker is a slang term for a computer enthusiast. Among professional programmers, the term hacker implies an amateur or a programmer who

lacks formal training. Depending on how it used, the term can be either complimentary or derogatory, although it is developing an increasingly derogatory connotation. The pejorative sense of hacker is becoming more prominent largely because the popular press has co-opted the term to refer to individuals who gain unauthorized access to computer systems for the purpose of stealing and corrupting data. Hackers, themselves, maintain that the proper term for such individuals is cracker.

Hard Disk

A hard disk contains a rotating magnetic media. Heads float over the surface of a disk, and read from the disk and write data to it.

Hardening

Hardening is the process of fixing vulnerabilities on a system. Hardening the system involves changing setting to help ensure the system is secure.

Hash Function

An algorithm that transforms a string of characters into a usually shorter value of a fixed length or a key that represents the original value.

Header

A header is the extra information in a packet that is needed for the protocol stack to process the packet.

Hijack Attack

A form of active wiretapping in which the attacker can seize control of a previously established communication association. Hijack attacks are similar to the-man-in the middle attack.

Home Page

The main page of a Website. Typically, the home page serves as an index or table of contents on the main page of a website.

Honeypot

A "honey pot" is a system intentionally place on a network with vulnerable points to act as a decoy/trap for unsuspecting hackers. The purpose of a honeypot can be to trap hackers or just to monitor their methods of attack.

Hops

A hop is a count between routers or gateways.

Host

The term "Host" typically refers to a server where websites reside.

HTTP Proxy

An HTTP proxy acts as an interacting service between HTTP clients (Web browsers) and HTTP served Web sites. These proxies can cache pages for faster retrieval. The program Squid, is a popular Linux based HTTP Proxy. www.squid-cache.org/

HTTPS

HTTPS in the URL, specifies that the use of HTTP enhanced by a security mechanism, which is usually SSL.

Hub

A Hub is a master station through which all communications to, from and between micro terminals must flow. A Hub typically works in a MESH network environment. Hubs rebroadcast signals to all ports.

Hybrid Dictionary Attack

A Hybrid Attack builds on the dictionary attack method by adding numerals and symbols to dictionary words. This type of attack is usually associated with a brute force password attack.

Hyperlink

In hypertext is an informational object (such as a word, or an image) within a webpage, that points to an area within the website or somewhere else on the Internet.

Hypertext Markup Language (HTML)

HTML is the coded language used to create a hypertext document for use on the Internet. Internet browsers translate the code into web pages and hypertext.

Hypertext Transfer Protocol (HTTP)

This protocol (port 80) is in the Internet Protocol (IP) family used to transport hypertext documents across an Internet.

I

Incident Handling

Incident Handling is a plan in dealing with intrusions, cyber-theft, denial of service, fire, floods, and other security-related events. It is comprised of a six-step process: **Preparation, Identification, Containment, Eradication, Recovery, and Lessons Learned.**

Incremental Backups
Incremental backups only backup the files that have been added or modified since the last backup.

IIS
Short for Internet Information Server, Microsoft's Web server that runs on Windows NT platforms. IIS comes bundled with Windows Server programs. Because IIS is tightly integrated with the operating system, it is relatively easy to administer.

Inetd (xinetd)
Inetd (or Internet Daemon) is an application that controls smaller Internet services like telnet, ftp, and POP in Unix and Linux systems.

Ingress Filtering
Ingress Filtering is the process of filtering inbound traffic.

Interrupt
An interrupt is a signal from a device that tells the computer that an event has occurred.

Input Validation Attacks
Input Validations Attacks are where an attacker intentionally sends unusual input in the hopes of confusing an application.

Internet
You're kidding me, right?

Internet Control Message Protocol (ICMP)
Internet Control Message Protocol (ICMP) is an extension to the Internet Protocol (IP) defined by RFC 792. ICMP supports packets containing error, control, and informational messages. The PING command, for example, uses ICMP to test an Internet connection.

Internet Engineering Task Force (IETF)

The body that defines standard Internet operating protocols such as TCP/IP. The IETF is supervised by the Internet Society Internet Architecture Board (IAB). IETF members are drawn from the Internet Society's individual and organization membership.

Internet Message Access Protocol (IMAP)
Internet Message Access Protocol, a protocol for retrieving e-mail messages. The latest version, IMAP4, is similar to POP3 but supports some additional features. For example, with IMAP4, you can search through your e-mail messages for keywords while the messages are still on the mail server.

Intranet
A network connecting computers within an organization using standard Internet protocols, esp. TCP/IP and HTTP.

Internet Protocol (IP)
The Internet Protocol, defined in STD 5, RFC 791, is the network layer for the TCP/IP Protocol Suite. It is a connectionless, best-effort packet switching protocol.

Intranet
An intranet computer network, usually a private network closed to outsiders.

Intrusion Detection
Intrusion detection is software used to detect attempted intrusion into a computer or network.

IP Address
An IP address is a unique 32-bit identifier for a computer or device that used on a TCP/IP network.

IP Flood
An example of an IP flood is a denial of service attack that sends a host more echo request ("ping") packets than the protocol implementation can handle.

IP Forwarding
IP forwarding allows a workstation or server to at as a router, and forward TCP/IP requests.

IPSec
Short for security, IPSec is a set of protocols developed to support the secure exchange of packets at the IP layer.

IP Spoofing
IP spoofing is a technique used to falsify the source IP Address of a hacker or another type of intruder.

ISDN
Integrated Services Digital Network, an international communications standard that allows ordinary phone lines to transmit digital instead of analogue signals, allowing data to be transmitted at a much faster rate than with a traditional modem.

ISO
International Organization for Standardization, a voluntary, non-treaty, non-government organization, established in 1947, with voting members that are designated standards bodies of participating nations and non-voting observer organizations.

ITU-T
International Telecommunications Union, Telecommunication Standardization Sector (formerly "CCITT"), a United Nations treaty organization that is composed mainly of postal, telephone, and telegraph authorities of the member countries and that publishes standards called "Recommendations."

J

Jabber
A jabbering node is a network device on an Ethernet network that is continuously sending data. This action is typically associated with a problem.

Jack

A jack is a female connector. (Should be called a Jane)

Jacket

The outer protective covering of a cable.

Java

An object orientated programming language designed to run on any computer platform or operating system. Java applets are sent as executable programs.

JavaScript

A scripting language that is sent as text and compiled on the client before execution.

Jitter

Jitter is the modification of fields in a database while preserving the aggregate characteristics.

Jump Drive

A jump drive is a small removable data storage device that uses flash memory and a USB connector.

Jumper

A jumper is a sleeve that bridges a circuit.

K

Kerberos

The authentication protocol implemented in DCE. Kerberos was developed at the Massachusetts Institute of Technology. The name comes from classical mythology, Kerberos was the three-headed dog that guarded the gates of the underworld.

Kernel

The Kernel is the center of a computer operating system, the core that provides basic services for all other parts of the operating system. Kernel and shell are typically terms used more frequently when describing the core of Unix and Linux.

L

L
Symbol used to designate inductance.

LAN
Local Area Network

LAN Adapter
Also called a Network Interface Card

Laser Printer
A printing device when out of paper, its user continues to print the same document several more times.

LATA
LATA is a telco term meaning, Local Access and Transport Area.

Layer 2 Forwarding Protocol (L2F)
An Internet protocol (originally developed by Cisco Corporation) that uses tunneling of PPP over IP to create a virtual extension of a dial-up link across a network, initiated by the dial-up server and transparent to the dial-up user.

Layer 2 Tunneling Protocol (L2TP)
An extension of the Point-to-Point Tunneling Protocol used by an Internet service provider to enable the operation of a virtual private network over the Internet.

Leased Line
A dedicated telephone line that is rented for exclusive 24-hours-a-day, 7-days-a-week use from one location to another.

Least Privilege
Least Privilege is the principle of allowing users or applications the least amount of permissions necessary to perform their intended function.

Lightweight Directory Access Protocol (LDAP)
Lightweight Directory Access Protocol. A protocol used to access a directory listing. Generally used in Web browsers and e-mail programs to enable lookups.

LILO
LILO is a commonly used bootstrap loader for Linux systems based on an Intel compatible processor.

Linux Torvalds
Creator of Linux while in college in 1991

Linux
A full featured and robust source operating system, similar to Unix.

Link State
Link state refers to route information from all routers linked with a geographic area,. The router uses this information to create a table of best-known routes.

Lobe
A lobe is an arm of a Token-ring with extends from a Multistation Access Unit.

LocalTalk
LocalTalk is Apple Computer's network scheme. LocalTalk uses a carrier sense multiple access with collision avoidance (CSMA/CA

Log Clipping
Log clipping is the removal of log entries from a system log to hide a compromise.

Longitudinal Coversion Loss (LCL)
Also called near-end unbalance attenuation, measures cable balance by comparing the signal appearing across the pair to the signal applied between ground and the pair, where the applied signal and the across pair signal are at the same end of the cable.

Longitudinal Coversion Transfer Loss (LCTL)

Also called far-end unbalance attenuation, measures cable balance by the comparison of the signal appearing across the pair to the signal between ground and the pair, where the applied signal is at the opposite end of the cable from where the across pair signal is measured.

Loopback
A type of diagnostic test in which a transmitted signal is returned to the sending device after passing through a data communications link or network.

Loopback Address
The loopback address (127.0.0.1) is a pseudo IP address from a properly configured network card that always refers back to the local host and are never sent out onto a network. To test if your local configuration is correct, it is standard to ping your loop back address.

M

M
Sign for Mutual Inductance

MAC Address
Media Access Control address is a unique physical address burned on each network device's network interface card.

Malicious Code
A Trojan horse is an example of Malicious Code. In code injected into a system without the users knowledge can be termed as malicious code.

Malware
Malware is a generic term used to generalize malicious code.

MAN
Metropolitan Area Network

Master Boot Record (MBR)
The master boot record, is the first logical sector on a disk where the BIOS to begin the bootstrap program.

Medium Access Control (MAC)
A device that operates at the data link layer of local area networks.

Morris Worm
A worm program written by Robert T. Morris, Jr. that flooded the ARPANET in November, 2 1988. Morris is now a professor at MIT.

Multi-Cast
Broadcasting from one host to multiple hosts.

Multi-Homed
Multi-homed typically refers to more than one NIC card on a computer, or can also refer to being directly connected to two or more ISP's.

Multiplexing
A multiplexed signal is a combined signal that is joined at its source and must be separated at its destination. Techniques that allow a number of simultaneous transmissions over a single circuit.

N

Name Space
DNS database structure.

Nerd
A term used to describe persons reading a book like this.

Netmask
Used by the TCP/IP protocol to decide how the network is broken up into sub-networks. For example, the network mask for a class C IP network is displayed as 0xffffff00, or 255.255.255.0.

Network Address Translation (NAT)
Network address translation (NAT) gives a company using a LAN the ability to protect their internal addresses from the Internet. NAT translates a public IP Address to a private one.

Network Mapping
To compile an inventory of the computer systems and the services on a network.

Network Taps
Network taps are devices that hook directly onto the network cable and can capture traffic.

Null Session
Known as Anonymous Logon, it is a way of letting an anonymous user retrieve information such as user names and shares over the network or connect without authentication. It is used by applications such as explorer.exe to enumerate shares on remote servers.

Octet
An octet is an eight-bit byte.

Open Shortest Path First (OSPF)
Open Shortest Path First is a link state routing algorithm used in interior gateway routing.

OSI layers
The 7-layer suite of protocols designed by ISO committees to be the international standard computer network architecture

Overload
A method to test a system component by placing excess performance on it.

Packet
Packet" a generic term used to describe unit of data at all levels of the protocol stack, but it is most correctly used to describe application data units. Also called a datagram.

Packet Switched Network
Packet switched networks are when individual packets follow their own paths through the network from one endpoint to another.

Partition
Division of a physical hard disk space.

Password Authentication Protocol (PAP)
Password Authentication Protocol is a simple, weak authentication mechanism where a user enters the password and it is then sent across the network in clear text.

Password Sniffing
Passive network tapping, (wiretapping) usually on a local area network, to gain knowledge of passwords. A network card on promiscuous mode can capture data on the wire and sniff out key words.

Patch
A patch is a bug fix released by a software manufacturer.

Payload
Payload is the actual application data a packet contains.

Penetration
Gaining unauthorized access to sensitive data by circumventing a system's protections. Also known as third base.

Penetration Testing
Penetration testing is used to test the external security of a remote station.

Permutation
Permutation keeps the same letters but changes the position within a text to scramble the message.

Personal Firewalls
Personal firewalls are those firewalls installed on individual PCs.

Phishing
"Phishing" is a form of identity theft by the act of sending email messages that are more or less exact copies of legitimate HTML emails from well-known companies. These e-mail are typically fake messages from banks, mortgage companies, or any other company that would ask you to input your SS number and personal records.

Ping of Death
The use of Ping with a packet size higher than 65,507. This will cause a denial of service.

Ping Sweep
An attack that sends ICMP echo requests ("pings") to a range of IP addresses, with the goal of finding hosts that can be probed for vulnerabilities.

Plaintext
Ordinary text before being encrypted.

Point-to-Point Protocol (PPP)
The Point-to-Point Protocol provides a method for transmitting packets over serial point-to-point links

Point-to-Point Tunneling Protocol (PPTP)
A VPN tunneling protocol uses one TCP port (for negotiation and authentication of a VPN connection) and one IP protocol (for data transfer) to connect the two nodes in a VPN.

Poison Reverse
Split horizon with poisoned reverse is how a routing protocol notifies neighboring routers that a route is no longer available. Since RIP allows up to 15 hops to another gateway, setting the hop count to 16 would mean "infinite."

Polyinstantiation
Polyinstantiation is the ability of a database to maintain multiple records with the same key.

Polymorphism
Polymorphism is the process by which malicious software changes its underlying code to avoid detection.

Port
In TCP/IP and UDP networks, a port is an endpoint to a logical connection. Only one process per machine can listen on the same port number.

Port Scan
A method an attacker uses to enumerate what services are running on your network. An attacker sends requests on different ports and takes note of which ports respond in certain way.

Post Office Protocol, Version 3 (POP3)
POP3 is a standard port used to receive e-mail.

Practical Extraction and Reporting Language (Perl)
A script programming language that is similar in syntax to the C language and that was made popular by Unix systems and then Linux.

Preamble
A preamble is a signal used in network communications to synchronize the transmission timing between two or more systems.

Pretty Good Privacy (PGP)
Trademark of Network Associates, Inc., PGP is the de facto standard for software encryption.

Private Addressing
IANA has set aside three address ranges for use by private or non-Internet connected networks. This is referred to as Private Address Space and is defined in RFC 1918. The reserved address blocks are: 10.0.0.0 to 10.255.255.255 (10/8 prefix) 172.16.0.0 to 172.31.255.255 (172.16/12 prefix) 192.168.0.0 to 192.168.255.255 (192.168/16 prefix)

Program Policy
A program policy is a high-level policy that sets the overall tone of an organization's security approach.

Promiscuous Mode
When a machine reads all packets off the network, regardless of who they are addressed to.

Proprietary Information
Proprietary information is information unique to a company and its ability to compete.

Protocol
A formal specification for communicating; an IP address the special set of rules that end points in a telecommunication connection use when they communicate.

Protocol Stack (OSI)
A group of drivers that work together to span the layers in the network protocol hierarchy.

Proxy Server

A security device that acts as an intermediary between a workstation and the Internet.

Public Key

A mathematically-derived code provided by a certificate authority.

R

Radiation Monitoring

Radiation monitoring is the process of receiving images, data, or audio from an unprotected source by listening to radiation signals.

Reconnaissance

Reconnaissance is the phase of an attack where "the" attackers finds new systems, maps out networks, and probes for specific, exploitable vulnerabilities.

Reflexive ACLs (Cisco)

Reflexive ACLs for Cisco routers are a step towards making the router act like a firewall. The router will make filtering decisions based on whether connections are a part of established traffic or not.

Registry

The Windows Registry is a database of systems configurations.

Reverse Address Resolution Protocol (RARP)

Reverse Address Resolution Protocol is a method of mapping the physical Ethernet address to the IP address of the host.

Reverse Engineering

The process of analyzing another subject's product or software, to identify and recreate it.

Reverse Lookup

A query in which the IP address is used to determine the DNS name for the computer.

Risk

Risk is the product of the level of threat with the level of vulnerability. It establishes the likelihood of a successful attack.

Risk Assessment

Risk assessment is the identification and quantification of the risk resulting from a specific use or occurrence.

Rivest-Shamir-Adleman (RSA)

An algorithm for asymmetric cryptography, invented in 1977 by Ron Rivest, Adi Shamir, and Leonard Adleman.

Root

Root is the name of the administrator account in Unix / Linux systems.

Rootkit

A collection of programs (and utilities) that a hacker uses to gain access to a system and obtain administrator-level.

Router

A router is a network appliance that interconnect logical networks by forwarding information to other networks based upon IP addresses.

Routing Information Protocol (RIP)

RIP is a distance vector protocol used for interior gateway routing which uses hop count to determine path costs.

Routing Loop

A routing loop is where two or more poorly configured routers repeatedly exchange redundant packets info.

RPC Scans

RPC scans determine which RPC services are running on a machine.

S

Scavenging

Searching through any accessible data to gain unauthorized knowledge of sensitive data.

Secure Shell (SSH)

Secure Shell is a command line interface used to securely access a remote computer. SSH is often the cause of many security problems.

Secure Sockets Layer (SSL)

A protocol developed by Netscape for transmitting private documents via the Internet.

Segment

Segment is another name for TCP packets.

Server

A server is a computer that handles requests for data, email, file transfers, and other network services from client computers

Session

A session is a virtual connection between two hosts by which network traffic is passed.

Session Hijacking

A method of attack, which involves a third party intercepting someone else's communications.

Session Key

In the context of symmetric encryption, a key that is temporary or is used for a relatively short period of time.

Shadow Password Files

An stored encrypted file with user passwords.

Share
A share is a resource made public on a machine, such as a directory (file share) or printer (printer share).

Shell
A Unix shell, also known as "the command line", provides the traditional user interface for the Unix and Linux operating systems. This is similar to Windows DOS prompt.

Simple Network Management Protocol (SNMP)
SNMP is a network management protocol used by network devices to exchange information.

Sniffer
A sniffer is a tool that monitors network traffic.

Social Engineering
Social engineering is the practice of conning people into revealing sensitive information regarding computer systems and passwords.

Socket
A socket is a combination of an IP address and port number that uniquely identifies a network service.

Spam
Electronic junk mail that usually involves penis enlargement and home refinancing.

Spanning Port
Configures the switch to behave like a hub for a specific port.

Spoofing
Impersonating another person or computer, usually by providing a false email name, URL or IP address.

SQL Injection
A type of exploit whereby hackers are able to execute SQL statements via an Internet browser

Stack Mashing
Stack mashing is the technique of using a buffer overflow to trick a computer into executing arbitrary code.

Static Host Tables
Static host tables are text files that contain hostname and address mapping.

Static Routing
Static routing means that routing table entries contain information that has been added manually and does not change.

Stealthing
Stealthing is a term that refers to approaches used by malicious code to conceal its presence on the infected system.

Steganalysis
Steganalysis is the process of detecting messages hidden using steganography.

Steganography
The process of hiding data inside other data.

Straight-Through Cable
A straight-through cable is where the pins on one side of the connector are wired to the same pins on the other end.

Subnet
An interconnected, but independent segment of a network that is identified by its Internet Protocol (IP) address.

Subnet Mask
32-bit address mask used in IP to indicate the bits of an IP address that are being used for the subnet address.

Switch

A switch is a networking device, similar to a hub, which keeps track of MAC addresses attached to each of its ports. In this way data is only transmitted to the ports of the intended recipient.

Switched Network

A communications network in which each user is connected to with a unique address, (such as a phone number or IP Address) that allows the system to connect two points together directly.

SYN Flood

A denial of service attack that sends a host TCP SYN packets that results in using up a systems resources so it cannot perform any other task.

Syslog

A program used to remotely record device logging.

System Security Officer (SSO)

A person responsible for the administration and enforcement of security policies to the system.

T1, T3

A digital circuit using TDM (Time-Division Multiplexing).

TCP Fingerprinting

TCP fingerprinting is a method of determining a remote operating system.

TCP/IP

Transmission Control Protocol/Internet Protocol (TCP/IP) is the basic communication protocol of the Internet. It can also be used as a communications protocol in a private network.

TELNET

A TCP-based program on the application-layer of the OSI model used for connecting to shells on remote network devices.

Threat Assessment
Process of evaluating the degree of threat to an information system and describing the nature of the threat.

Time to Live
An Internet header field which indicates the upper bound on how long this Internet datagram may exist.

Token Ring
A token ring network is a local area network in which all computers are connected in a ring or star topology. A token-passing scheme is used in order to prevent the collision of data between computers that want to send messages at the same time.

Topology
The geometric configuration of a computer network, or how the network is physically laid out. Common topologies are star (centralized), bus (decentralized), and ring (decentralized).

Trunking
Trunking is connecting switches together with multiple ports to allow more data to pass.

Unicast
Broadcasting from host to host.

Uniform Resource Identifier (URI)
The generic term for all types of names and addresses that refer to objects on the World Wide Web.

Uniform Resource Locator (URL)
A unique identifier used on the World Wide Web to locate websites and web pages. www.thenetworkadministrator.com is a URL.

Unix
A popular operating system, developed by AT&T in 1969, that was very important in the development of the Internet. UNIX allows more than one user to access a computer system at the same time. An early version of

UNIX, which was used by most colleges and universities, incorporated TCP/IP and made Internet connections possible.

Unprotected Share
In Windows terminology, a "share" is a mechanism that allows a user to connect to file systems and printers on other systems. An "unprotected share" is one that allows anyone to connect to it.

Users
A term used to describe those peoples that live in and around the Hollywood CA, area. <u>Also a term used for computer users.</u>

User Contingency Plan
User contingency plan is the alternative methods of continuing operations if computer systems are unavailable.

User Datagram Protocol (UDP)
User Datagram Protocol. A connectionless unreliable protocol. UDP describes a network data connection based on datagrams with little packet control.

Virtual Private Network (VPN)
(Virtual Private Network) -- Usually refers to a network in which some of the parts are connected using the public Internet, but the data sent across the Internet is encrypted, so the entire network is "virtually" private.

Vulnerability
What happens to a network when boredom sets in to the IT department.

WAN
Wide Area Network

War Dialer
A computer program that automatically dials a series of telephone numbers to find lines connected to computer systems.

War Driving
War driving is the process of driving around searching for wireless access points that are open.

WHOIS
An IP for finding information about resources on networks.

WIN32
A Window's application programming interface (API)

Windump
Windump is a freeware protocol analyzer for Windows that monitors network traffic on a wire.

Wired Equivalent Privacy (WEP)
Wireless Equivalent Privacy. Compression used in WiFi networks. Exists in two different security levels, 40(64) bit and 128 bit encryption. The higher the bit number, the more secure the encryption.

Wireless Application Protocol (WAP)
A specification for a set of communication protocols to standardize the way that wireless devices, such as cellular telephones and radio transceivers, can be used for Internet access, including e-mail, the World Wide Web, newsgroups, and Internet Relay Chat.

Wiretapping
Also known as The Man in the Middle, wiretapping is placing a computer or device on a network to record data.

Worm
A computer program that independently propagates into computer systems.

Wrap
To use cryptography to provide data confidentiality service for a data object. Also, music that rhymes badly.

XML

Extensible Markup Language, is used to define documents with XML compatible programs.

Y2K

Year 2000. A term used in 1999, to scare businesses into upgrading their computer equipment. Also called the Millennium Bug, when the year 2000 rolled over many older programs was not programmed to rollover from 1999 to 2000. Many people predicted doom, nuclear holocaust, and Armageddon. Those that survived Y2K—everyone—are currently spending their time on more practical disasters such as meteoric impacts on the earth.

Yottabyte

A yottabyte is 2 to the 80th power, or
1,208,925,819,614,629,174,706,176 bytes

Zettabyte

A zettabyte is 2 to the 70th power, or 1,180,591,620,717,411,303,424 bytes.

ZIP

A zip file is a compressed filed for Windows based computers.